TAROT AS YOU FLOW

This Guidebook and Journal Belongs to:

_____

COPYRIGHT © 2021 BY LOWELLA F. - ALL RIGHTS RESERVED.

The content contained within this book may not be reproduced, duplicated or transmitted without direct written permission from the author or the publisher, Mystical Garden, except where permitted by law.

Legal Notice:

This book is copyright protected. This book is only for personal use. You cannot amend, distribute, sell, use, quote or paraphrase any part, or the content within this book, without the consent of the author or publisher.

Disclaimer Notice:

Please note the information contained within this document is for educational purposes only. No warranties of any kind are declared or implied. Readers acknowledge that the author is not engaging in the rendering of legal, financial, medical or professional advice.

By reading this document, the reader agrees that under no circumstances is the author responsible for any losses, direct or indirect, which are incurred as a result of the use of the information contained within this book.

* The card images used in this book are taken from the Rider-Waite Tarot deck, drawn by illustrator Pamela Colman Smith from the instructions of academic and mystic A. E. Waite. The Rider-Waite Tarot deck artwork is part of the public domain.

Contents

Introduction 1

Spread 2

Shuffling 4

Drawing 5

The Major Arcana 6

The Minor Arcana

    Swords 50

    Wands 78

    Pentacles 106

    Cups 134

Helpful Points 162

Final Tips 163

Notes 164

"The true Tarot is symbolism; it speaks no other language and offers no other signs."

— A. E. WAITE

Introduction

Discover Tarot in a simple, relatable, straightforward and practical way with Tarot As You Flow Guidebook and Journal! Far from clichés of conceptual abstractions, generic advice or anything too philosophical, this book presents individual card indications in bullet format which allows for easier learning and recall and serves as a quick yet substantial reference material, with spaces provided for readers to jot down added notes or info as desired.

Tarot is a tool that sheds light on the truth of things and helps one gain insight or better understanding on the situation in question. It can be used for divination, reflection, guidance and of course, fun! Got any question, problem, uncertainty or curiosity? Whip out your deck and find out what the cards have to say! Tarot does not deny free will however. The purpose of Tarot is to get a reading based on current energies and unveil potential possibilities or the most likely outcome.

Through this book, you'll learn how to read Tarot in a grounded way, understand or grasp each card's meaning (upright and reversed) or what they are trying to represent, learn an uncomplex, straightforward yet effective spread and get to know my shuffling/drawing method of choice. It is my hope that this journal proves to be a considerably helpful learning tool that allows you to get a handle on and connect with the cards more easefully, making for a convenient resource that enables you to start reading quickly, develop interpretation skills fast and achieve a notable level of familiarity with the powerful Tarot, building your intuition, confidence and abilities as you go! :)

Spread

I personally like things simple, direct and uncomplicated. But of course I am not against other more complex spreads. Please feel free to look into other sources for other types of spreads. What I'm going to present here is the one I use, which is a 3-card spread that is "expoundable".

Example, a reading for (name) in terms of her job or career:

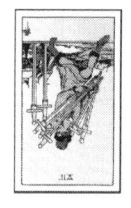

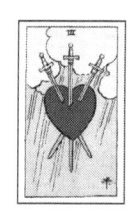

Now by pulling these 3 cards, we can already get a sense of the essence of the situation we're doing the reading about. 7 of Swords reversed indicates wanting to separate self from the job, feeling like it's not worth it ("these swords" turned out to be not worth it). It looks to be a stressful/upsetting/dissatisfying job (3 of Swords) and the querent is wanting/trying to move to a better place (The Devil reversed).

If we would like context or clarification for each card drawn, we can pull more cards to clarify or "expound" on each 'pile' in order to further reveal the picture:

Spread

Through pulling more cards, we find out that the querent wants to be somewhere else but is feeling a sense of stuckness, not knowing what to do (8 of Swords), and this could very well be a cyclic pattern (6 of Cups reversed) that's been going on for her. 4 of Pentacles reversed and 7 of Cups reversed explains the stressful work condition - feeling a sense of insecurity or lack of control and feeling overwhelmed. The 3rd pile as we can see is all about trying to get to a better place. 2 of Wands reversed and Knight of Pentacles reversed indicates that the job does not feel to be in alignment with the querent, things are not working well for her and it's time to figure out something else. The High Priestess calls for tuning into one's own intuition and inner wisdom/guidance. Perhaps look more into fields that involve creation or using creativity (The Empress). And finally the Knight of Cups encourages to listen to the heart, move forward in a way that is in alignment with one's heart or take action on what naturally feels right and alive for oneself.

Another way I do it is to lay out a 3-card spread, and after reading that, if more information or clarification is needed/desired, I just pull more sets of 3. Stop when you feel it's done or when you've already got what you can get out of the reading. And that's it!

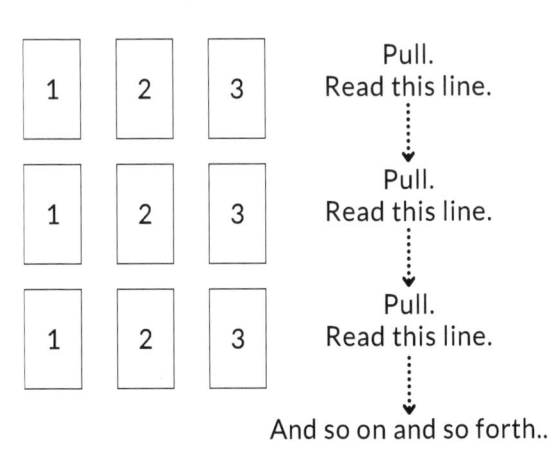

1	2	3	Pull. Read this line.
1	2	3	Pull. Read this line.
1	2	3	Pull. Read this line.

And so on and so forth..

Shuffling

If you're like me, you want to preserve the integrity of the cards as much as possible. Yes, you can shuffle the cards the way you'd shuffle a poker deck, however, that may wear out the cards more quickly. The way I shuffle is to 'scramble' the cards on the table:

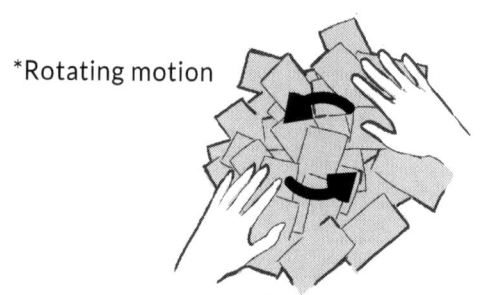

*Rotating motion

*Note: This is the time to ask your question or have in mind the event/situation you are doing a reading on.

After 'scrambling' the cards on the table, gather them up into a deck. Hold the cards across your left palm and continue to shuffle the cards by taking a chunk from the back and placing them at the front.

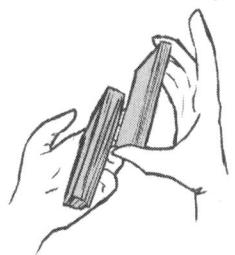

With your left thumb, slide the topmost cards down while you lift the remaining chunk and again, bring it to the front, holding lightly, allowing the topmost cards to be 'taken' by the left thumb. Repeat this motion until the chunk of cards is 'consumed'.

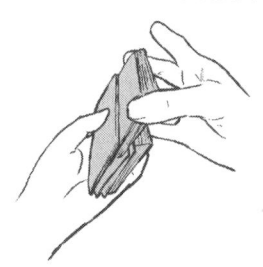

In a rapid manner, rinse and repeat this shuffling technique of taking from the back and bringing to the front with sliding and lifting motion until satisfied.

Drawing

There are a few ways of drawing cards. You can simply pick the ones on top, or spread the cards across the table and choose the ones you're drawn to pick. The way I do it, is what resonates with me the most, I find. So this is my personal choice of how to draw cards:

Once I feel the cards are shuffled enough, using the same motion, I take a portion of the back and drop (or gently throw) it at the front. You'll notice that there'll be a card that's going to jut out the most. That's the one to take. If there is not one card that obviously protrudes the most, just repeat the motion.

*Sticks out the most

You'll notice that it's usually the bottommost card that will poke out. So you may ask why not just take the bottom card, cut the deck in 2, and place the bottom chunk on top and repeat? Well, it's much easier, more seamless and fun this way. Also, sometimes a card may 'accidentally' drop, and I take that as a sign that's the card to take. If 2 or more cards drop, I don't consider those and put them back in the deck and proceed with the back to front dropping motion to get a card.

And that's it! Enjoy!

The Fool

◆ UPRIGHT ◆

INNOCENCE, CAUGHT OFF GUARD
FREEDOM, NOT LETTING SOMETHING GET IN THE WAY
SPONTANEITY, LEAP OF FAITH
YOUTH

◆ INDICATIONS ◆

- Kids/about childhood; youth/child card
- Taking a leap of faith; "I'm gonna do what I'm gonna do"; being ready to be all in and fully jump into something
- Spontaneity; foolishness; adventurous; being young and free; free spirit
- "Screw it, let me just make a power move in a forward direction"; not letting something get in the way
- New journey
- Caught off guard, surprised, wasn't expecting it
- A person who played dumb and naive

◆ NOTES ◆

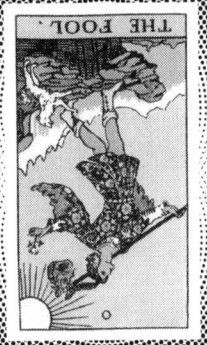

The Fool

◆ REVERSE ◆

RECKLESSNESS, CARELESSNESS
FOOLISH, RASH OR OVERLY IMPULSIVE CHOICES
HOLDING BACK, UNABLE TO BE SPONTANEOUS
SERIOUS, MATURE, NOT NAIVE

◆ INDICATIONS ◆

- Not able to be spontaneous; clinging to the old; fear of the unknown
- A call to not be naive
- Growing up; not naive; being serious and mature, maturity
- A serious situation; a serious time
- Something reckless; actions that are rash and reckless
- Something messed up in one's childhood

◆ NOTES ◆

The Magician

◆ UPRIGHT ◆

FOCUS, WILLPOWER, CONTROL
MANIFESTATION, RESOURCEFULNESS
PREPARATION, INTENTIONALITY
ACCESSING OR UTILIZATION OF AVAILABLE TOOLS FOR ONE'S AGENDA

◆ INDICATIONS ◆

- Card of talent and power; making the most out of your tools and abilities
- "I can make this into whatever I need it to be"; presenting your case; showing the audience what you want them to see
- Able to find a way to gather resources together and make something of it; using all the resources you have or can get to your advantage
- People that have access to resources, have all the stuff you need to get stuff done; being very resourceful, can pull things together; having a lot of networks/connections
- Preparing, somebody who's about to take or taking things into their own hands; gonna have more things coming out of their sleeves
- People trying to lead us into believing something but it's actually something else (also reverse)

◆ NOTES ◆

The Magician

◆ REVERSE ◆

MANIPULATION, MISDIRECTION, ILLUSION
ABUSE OF POWER/RESOURCES
COMMUNICATION ISSUES (POOR, INCORRECT, BLOCKED, ETC.)
NOT HAVING OR LACKING RESOURCES

◆ INDICATIONS ◆

- The Magician is a very mercurial card, which rules communications, communications like media, publications, communications between 2 people/entities, etc (also upright)
- Problem with communication: saying something we try to hide, saying something you shouldn't; can also be about being quiet, like things done in silence (e.g., in terms of generating income, acquiring resources, etc.)
- Poor communication skills; something going wrong with communications or communication issues: inaccurate information; not being heard, etc.
- Things said were calculated and serve as a misdirection/manipulation
- What's been told to the world/public is not correct
- A narcissistic, controlling or manipulative person; improper use of power/resources
- Taking people's resources away, suppressing someone's ability to speak
- Not having the right amount of resources (to prove, defend self etc.); not fully prepared and able to do something yet

◆ NOTES ◆

The High Priestess

◆ UPRIGHT ◆

HIDDEN KNOWLEDGE, SECRECY
EUREKA MOMENTS, INSIGHTS
INTUITION, KNOWING
TRUSTWORTHINESS AND DEPENDABILITY

◆ INDICATIONS ◆

- Intuition, gut sense; realizing e.g., what should be done, what kind of innovations we need, who do we approach and who do we not, etc.
- Receptivity to insights; eureka/awakening moments; knowing; "the person knew"; seeing what works and what doesn't; what should be a priority
- Dependability, trustworthiness; someone one trusts/trusted; truth and honesty; being authentic to what has happened
- Middle path/middle pillar; the highest good; being in tune (with inner wisdom, divine timing, with one another, etc.)
- Secret knowledge, hidden/deeper/universal/divine knowledge; mystery; higher power
- Secrets, things being secretive and happening on the low; may also indicate back channel (also reverse)

◆ NOTES ◆

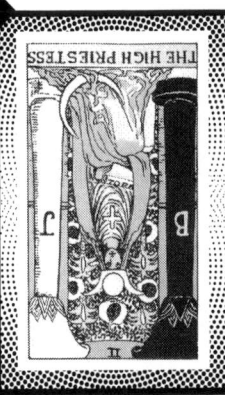

The High Priestess

◆ REVERSE ◆

KEEPING SECRETS FOR ILL INTENTIONS
LACK OF INTEGRITY, UNTRUSTWORTHY
BAD VIBES, HIDDEN AGENDAS
DISCONNECTED FROM ONE'S TRUTH AND INTUITION

◆ INDICATIONS ◆

- Disconnected from intuition or not listening to it; bad timing, issues with timing; breaking of connection with inner knowing/voice
- Having a bit of a difficult time getting connected to Self; can indicate not really knowing (something)
- Distrust; distrustful character; breaking of trust
- Not entirely honest; not entirely full of integrity or having poor integrity; not dependable; morality problem
- The High Priestess is a card of spirituality and wisdom, intuition and trusting your higher power, when reversed, it means don't trust the situation being provided to you; mistruths
- Untrustworthy; ill intent; projecting the wrong image; someone who is manipulating the story; things are not what they seem; hidden secrets, keeping secrets; hidden agendas
- May sometimes indicate times are changing (upturned pillars)

◆ NOTES ◆

The Empress

◆ UPRIGHT ◆

MATERNAL ENERGY, IN CHARGE

NURTURING

FERTILE ENERGY, GIVING BIRTH (LITERALLY OR FIGURATIVELY)

CREATIVITY AND CREATION

◆ INDICATIONS ◆

- Pregnant woman; fertile energy (e.g., let's start nurturing something); fertility card of circumstance, like being able to really plant and nourish the seeds you want to grow in your own life; prolific creation
- New life; new life is starting; new way of life
- Maternal protector energy; mother figure; a nurturing figure; someone you feel strongly attached to; warm nurturing presence
- Can represent someone who is majorly responsible for the situation; someone who is in charge of something; nurtures others in something
- Powerful female, knows what she's doing; strong prominent female figure; can represent the wife

◆ NOTES ◆

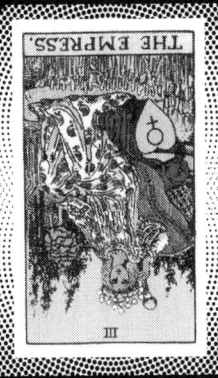

The Empress

◆ REVERSE ◆

LACK OF FEMININE ENERGY
LACKING OR EXCESSIVE NURTURING, LACK OF INVESTMENT
FERTILITY ISSUES, SEEDS NOT GROWING
NOT EMPOWERED

◆ INDICATIONS ◆

- Not being able to grow the seeds you want to grow; fertility issues
- Lack of investment
- Missing mother figure; mother issues
- Not empowered, coming from a victim mentality; lack of self love or self care
- Loss of control; not in complete control, e.g., she has no idea what was going on until the issue/situation happened/exploded
- Can also indicate change in leadership
- Overly nurturing (like, too mom); can indicate helicopter parenting
- Someone abusing her power; abusive control; can be taking advantage of feminine power
- Too masculine, lack of feminine energy
- Someone younger

◆ NOTES ◆

The Emperor

◆ UPRIGHT ◆

A FATHER FIGURE, AUTHORITY
STABILITY, DEPENDABILITY, STRUCTURE
POWER, CONTROL
A PERSON OR ENTITY WHO'S IN CHARGE

◆ INDICATIONS ◆

- Paternal figure; serious; mature; in a powerful position; has status; authority
- Someone who's supposed to distribute all the fruits evenly
- Someone who has high standing in a work environment, like a boss or manager; dealings with authority figures
- Someone/an organization who's in charge, like the company people are working under
- Power figure; in control, in charge; the mastermind; someone/the entity who has control (e.g., the management, corporation, etc.)
- Total control, absolute power
- Autonomy; masculine energy; taking action; solidly moving forward with ambition
- Establishing something and bringing it forward

◆ NOTES ◆

The Emperor

◆ REVERSE ◆

DOMINATION, EXCESSIVE CONTROL
POWER ABUSE, AUTHORITY WITH NO GOOD INTENTIONS
PATERNAL ISSUES
KNOCKED OFF THE THRONE

◆ INDICATIONS ◆

- Unchecked power; rigidity; tyrannical; oppressive
- High authority who does not have our best interest at heart: corrupt, lack of discipline or fairness, knowing some things and not telling the people for his own agendas, etc.
- Insanely manipulative; power trip; abusing power
- Controlling; dominating; not having good intentions
- Can indicate wanting to knock someone off the throne; someone knocked off the throne
- Absentee father; pretend dad; paternity issues
- Going too far in terms of being driven or ambitious

◆ NOTES ◆

The Hierophant

◆ UPRIGHT ◆

COMMITMENT, FOLLOW-THROUGH, MARRIAGE
TRADITION, RELIGION, BELIEFS
STATUS QUO, ORGANIZATION, INSTITUTION
EDUCATION, KNOWLEDGE

◆ INDICATIONS ◆

- Some kind of entity/organization running the show; establishment/institutions type card
- Commitment, follow through
- Marriage; commitment, e.g., someone/people/friends/etc. the person is committed to
- Religious activities, ceremonies, rituals; religious values; doing things the traditional way
- Established system, structure, status quo, rules
- Going with the plan, following the steps
- Learning and knowledge
- Some kind of mediation outside of going to court

◆ NOTES ◆

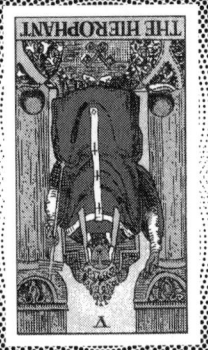

The Hierophant

◆ REVERSE ◆

LACK OF COMMITMENT OR FOLLOW-THROUGH
UNCONVENTIONALITY, NON-CONFORMITY
NOT ACCORDING TO THE BOOK/STRUCTURE/SYSTEM
INSTITUTION OR ORGANIZATION HAVING ILL INTENTIONS

◆ INDICATIONS ◆

- Don't expect much follow through
- Breaking of commitment; lack of commitment; problem with following through
- Issues within marriage, cutting ties
- Suppression from management, e.g.," you can't do this, this isn't a good look, this isn't on brand", etc.
- Establishment/institution/organization having bad/malevolent intentions
- Institution at a disadvantaged position
- Non-traditional thing; non-standard way
- Old systems or structures crumbling
- Letting go of the old (way of thinking, dogma, tradition, etc.)
- Old connection, old commitment

◆ NOTES ◆

The Lovers

◆ UPRIGHT ◆

LOVE, UNIONS
PARTNERSHIPS, RELATIONSHIPS
STABLE BUSINESS
SHARED VALUES, PRINCIPLES OR GOALS

◆ INDICATIONS ◆

- Partnerships, relationships, connections
- Union; getting back together; stable romantic/business/platonic relationship
- Like-minded people
- Motive is to get close to people
- Can indicate the person is involved in the situation
- Doing business; making deals/agreements; depending on other cards, can be dirty dealings like paying people off, etc. (also reverse)

◆ NOTES ◆

The Lovers

◆ REVERSE ◆

DISHARMONY, CONFLICT, TRUST ISSUES
DISCONNECTION, DISUNION, DETACHMENT
BUSINESS/AGREEMENT GOING SOUTH
BAD BUSINESS DECISIONS OR PRACTICES

◆ INDICATIONS ◆

- Breaking of some sort of connection or relationship
- Imbalanced partnership; disharmony; arguing a lot; fallout (doesn't have to be a romantic relationship)
- Decisions and agreements that fall through, like a friend who's not going to come through; disagreement between 2 people
- Breaking of agreement in some way
- In terms of business stuff, things not looking so great; business/career breaking down
- Business/agreement going south; bad business/career decisions; bad business practices like blackmail, bribery, etc.
- Can indicate someone being separated from the person they are with at that time
- Can mean we have to be careful about the people around us (e.g., untrustworthy connections, people leaking things, etc.)

◆ NOTES ◆

The Chariot

◆ UPRIGHT ◆

SUCCESS, DIRECTED WILLPOWER
CONTROL, DIRECTION
MOVEMENT, PROGRESS
TRAVEL, ESCAPE

◆ INDICATIONS ◆

- Harnessing or gathering opposing/ conflicting forces (Yin Yang) and moving them in the same direction
- Things are progressing; moving ahead with confidence; taking the reigns and going somewhere with them
- Forward-moving energy; action; having courage and staying focused on the road ahead; heading towards something
- Related to traveling or trafficking
- Moving on; also escape route
- Pulling self together; directed willpower; mission; movement; victory
- Can indicate something is going along just fine; can also mean yes, we/they are going to try or go for it

◆ NOTES ◆

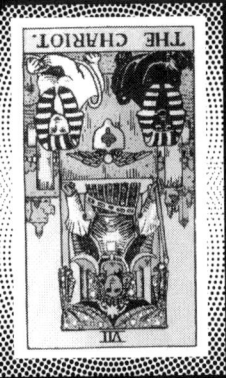

The Chariot

◆ REVERSE ◆

INTERRUPTION OR HALT IN PROGRESS
BEING BLOCKED BY OBSTACLES
SCATTERED OR CONFLICTING ENERGY
AIMLESSLY CHARGING AHEAD, NEED FOR DIRECTION/FOCUS

◆ INDICATIONS ◆

- Sudden interruption
- Halt in progress, halting of progress
- Energy being halted
- Things kinda had to stop, to pause/stop something
- Hold your horses, pump the break
- Shutting something down
- Aimless; lacking directionality; the need to pull self/forces together; the need to focus your energy
- Travel issues; unable to escape

◆ NOTES ◆

Strength

◆ UPRIGHT ◆

STRENGTH, INNER POWER
SELF-CONTROL, TAMING
PATIENCE, FORTITUDE
STUBBORNNESS, ENDURANCE, HISTORY

◆ INDICATIONS ◆

- Having or regaining control of oneself; softness and inner power/strength; calmness in the face of uncertainty
- Patience; fortitude; in a strong spot/position
- We are stronger than we realize; we are more capable than we think
- Can indicate having something/things going for you
- Stubbornness, strong, stern
- They have history of doing this
- This has been going on forever; been going on for a while or been sitting on it for a long time; something long-running
- Can indicate taming the animal desires; a call to not be pulled like a dog on a leash by every primitive egoic whim, itch, reactivity and desire and instead have sovereignty over one's self; it's up to you
- Sometimes this card can also represent taking control and shutting something down, e.g., wanting someone to shut up, etc. (represented by the card image of a woman trying to close the lion's mouth)

◆ NOTES ◆

Strength

◆ REVERSE ◆

WEAK SPOT OR POSITION
NEED TO PLACE ENERGY OR PERSEVERANCE ELSEWHERE
INSECURITY, FEAR
VULNERABLE

◆ INDICATIONS ◆

- Fear takes over; insecure; struggles for control or autonomy
- Spending a lot of energy; something that is not your 'strength'
- In a weak spot/situation
- Finding your vulnerabilities; being honest and vulnerable
- Can indicate catching someone when they are vulnerable; "I'm exposing your vulnerable spots."
- Being pulled/led by the lizard part of your brain; self-destructive impulses

◆ NOTES ◆

The Hermit

◆ UPRIGHT ◆

ISOLATION, SOLITUDE
WITHDRAWAL, QUIET
HOLDING BACK
INNER REFLECTION, CONTEMPLATION

◆ INDICATIONS ◆

- Keeping to your own; staying in your own lane; keeping quiet, keeping things hush hush
- Keeping something close to the vest; pulling inside
- Things kept back/held back (from the public, etc.)
- There are things they are keeping secret or hiding (that caused this situation, put them or others in this position, etc.)
- Isolation, feeling isolated/withdrawn and on your own; wanting to isolate (someone)
- Somebody ghosting somebody; have withdrawn energy from an individual or group; pulled away (from people you're collaborating with, etc.)
- One-sided
- A call for meditation to gain wisdom
- Can indicate unexpectedly quiet response; no one paid attention; no one is bothered; crickets

◆ NOTES ◆

The Hermit

············◆ **REVERSE** ◆············

PULLED OUT OF COMFORT ZONE
COMING OUT OF ISOLATION
RESISTING INTROSPECTION, DISTRACTING SELF
FORCED WITHDRAWAL

············◆ **INDICATIONS** ◆············

- Getting out of our comfort zone; getting out of our house; pulled out of comfort zone or the house; people who in the past haven't really come forward/been out and about, are gonna start wanting to come out/forward, say/do something
- Coming out of isolation
- Not taking the time to chill and reflect
- Didn't want to deal with something, distracting self with other things to get away from this problem; resistance to self-honesty or contemplation
- Can also indicate the extremes of solitude; Pulling away; not wanting to be out there/known/seen, being in some form of hiding
- Forced withdrawal; not having a choice but to hold things back; forcibly isolated in some way; unable to be completely honest about some things, couldn't say things, not allowed to speak; hands tied

············◆ **NOTES** ◆············

The Wheel of Fortune

◆ UPRIGHT ◆

GOOD LUCK, GOOD OPPORTUNITY
DESTINY, FATE
CHANGE, A TURN OF EVENTS, MOVEMENT
KARMA, CYCLES OF LIFE

◆ INDICATIONS ◆

- A turn of events; things change; karmic situation/lesson; wheels turn; things can turn at any time
- Good luck and fate
- A really good opportunity, like a lucky break, a big deal move, someone cashing in on something/someone, etc.
- Momentum is gathering
- Can indicate there are other opportunities; a better opportunity; can mean ended up getting the opportunity/stuff elsewhere
- Something divinely planned, something fated/destined to happen; unavoidable; if upright, it's a good thing, if reversed, not (at least, not in terms of the limited human sense)
- Train has already left the station, fated type of thing
- Divine law
- Time, outgrowing something
- Can indicate if something is let go, things are going to move forward in a good way; a call to surrender to what is and what will be

◆ NOTES ◆

The Wheel of Fortune

◆ REVERSE ◆

BAD LUCK
OPPORTUNITY TAKEN AWAY
UNWELCOME CHANGES, A DOWNTURN
RISK NOT WORTH TAKING

◆ INDICATIONS ◆

- Opportunity taken away; golden opportunity ripped away
- "You promised me something and you didn't give it to me"
- Bad luck; bad opportunity; unlucky situation to get wrapped up in
- Risk not worth taking
- Bad news that's fated to happen; something's coming that you can't really escape or prevent from happening
- A downturn; if you've been doing something you're not supposed to be doing, it is time to pay your dues; karma comes calling

◆ NOTES ◆

Justice

◆ UPRIGHT ◆

JUSTICE, FAIRNESS
CAUSE AND EFFECT
LAW, LEGAL MATTERS
INTEGRITY, TRUTH

◆ INDICATIONS ◆

- Court manners; judicial system; striving for balance/fairness
- Some kind of legality involved; legalities; the justice system; police
- Seeking justice in a legal situation
- What's fair is fair; objectivity; integrity
- Cause and effect card; consequences
- The truth that needs to come out
- Legal reward
- if beside Ace of Pentacles reverse, indicates threatening to sue

◆ NOTES ◆

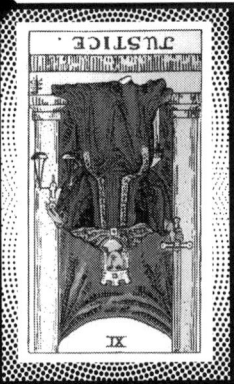

Justice

◆ REVERSE ◆

INJUSTICE, UNFAIRNESS
DISHONESTY, CORRUPTION
AVOIDANCE OR LACK OF ACCOUNTABILITY
NEGATIVE KARMA

◆ INDICATIONS ◆

- Illegal, unjust and unfair; doing things that are unjust
- Feeling the blame; feeling guilty for the situation
- Being treated unfairly; getting ripped off
- Poetic justice; harsh justice; harsh legal battles; truth of the matter coming to bite you in the behind
- Justice delayed is justice denied; dirty court shenanigans
- Not willing to take full accountability; trying to 'dodge the bullet' and blame others

◆ NOTES ◆

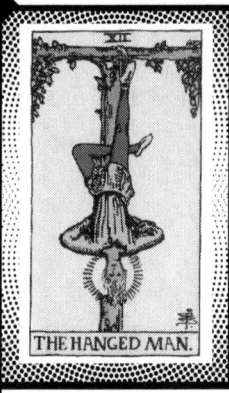

The Hanged Man

◆ UPRIGHT ◆

SACRIFICE, LETTING GO
ACCEPTANCE, SURRENDER
WAITING, DELAYS, CONTEMPLATION
PERSPECTIVE CHANGE

◆ INDICATIONS ◆

- Waiting; pauses; suspension; time out; a hold up; delays; trying to figure out what's gonna happen
- Debating about something; sitting on something
- Hasn't happened yet; something that's (still) up in the air
- Needing to put yourself in a timeout
- Perspective change
- Surrender; needing to let go; having to let go of something or someone
- Acceptance; something that you'll just have to accept; can also be thinking about how you'll be accepted
- This was under consideration for longer than what people might have expected; someone considering something (this change, this move, etc.) for a while
- Sacrifice; cutting out

◆ NOTES ◆

The Hanged Man

······················◆ **REVERSE** ◆······················

NOT LETTING GO
RESISTING ACCEPTANCE
INTENTIONALLY DRAGGING SOMETHING FOR AS LONG AS POSSIBLE
FORCED TO ACCEPT

············◆ **INDICATIONS** ◆············

- Slightly isolated; not letting go, some sort of grudge
- We're not gonna let go of it; not letting something go; won't let someone let go
- Holding on for dear life; feeling like a victim; "I have an axe to grind with you, I won't let go."
- Old stuff resurfacing; old drama that hasn't been let go of
- Just having to accept/come to terms with something (though not wanting to); not wanting to let go of something but being forced to let go of it
- Unduly lengthy pauses or delays, dragging something for as long as possible
- Something that has been a long time coming

············◆ **NOTES** ◆············

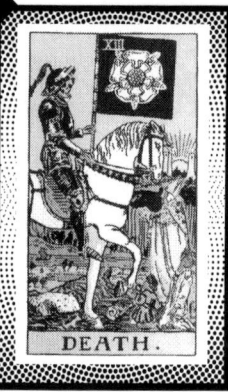

Death

⧫ UPRIGHT ⧫

ENDINGS
CHANGE, TRANSFORMATION
TRANSITION
RELEASE, DISCARD

⧫ INDICATIONS ⧫

- Ending; transformation; release

- A huge change; transition; end of a chapter

- A change that's going to befall the person; in order for growth to take place, the outworn must be discarded

- A call to adapt, change, do something different

- Wishing something would end and transition into something else

- Scorpionic energy (mysterious and secretive in their ways)

- Putting an end to one individual

⧫ NOTES ⧫

Death

◆ REVERSE ◆

NOT OVER

RESISTING CHANGE

HANGING ON TO "DEAD" THINGS WAY PAST THEIR "EXPIRATION DATE"

ACCIDENTAL DEATH, NOT READY

◆ INDICATIONS ◆

- Situation that's not over; this isn't over, there's still more to come
- Holding on for dear life; resisting change; not wanting to let go or move on
- Holding on to something and not letting it end when it needs to end; things that needed to end but haven't exactly ended (the way that they should)
- What's going on can't keep going
- Pushing something past its lifespan, like a long time coming thing
- Accidental death; "I wasn't ready"

◆ NOTES ◆

Temperance

◆ UPRIGHT ◆

BALANCE, GIVE AND TAKE, PATIENCE
ALCHEMY
PURPOSE, TIMING
'TRANSFER' OF INFO OR GOSSIP

◆ INDICATIONS ◆

- Patience; balance; having to be patient and balanced; being calm and collected, waiting; bide your time
- Rebalancing; restructuring
- Fairness; universal balance, reaping what you've sown
- Life passion; purpose; higher power and timing; go with the flow
- Give and take
- Harmony; moderation; can represent health, healing, sobriety
- Alchemy; can sometimes indicate planning something in the shadows; mixing/blending something in the background; be careful of a wolf wearing a sheep's clothing
- Exchange of information; gossip, people knowing

◆ NOTES ◆

Temperance

◆ REVERSE ◆

OUT OF BALANCE, IMPATIENCE
OFF-PURPOSE, NOT THE RIGHT TIMING
'FORMULA' NOT WORKING
PREVENTING GOSSIP OR LEAK OF INFO

◆ INDICATIONS ◆

- Impatience; imbalance
- Not waiting
- Not the right timing, timing is against us/them
- Disharmony; not in line with purpose, off-path, off-mission, off-purpose; not wanting things to get up on the path the way they should
- Not tempering well; what is 'mixed' or concocted is not really working
- 'Unbalanced blend'; a need to practice moderation in some aspects of your life
- Not fair, e.g., feeling like I did more for you than you did for me
- Disrupted/slowed flow or pace
- Blocked flow of information; we don't want anyone talking and gossiping

◆ NOTES ◆

The Devil

◆ UPRIGHT ◆

BONDAGE, MATERIALISM
NEGATIVITY, SLAVERY
OPPRESSION, ADDICTION, EXCESS
INTERNAL STRUGGLES, MENTAL HEALTH ISSUES

◆ INDICATIONS ◆

- Imbalance, scales being out of whack; bondage; excess
- Can represent addictions like sex or substance use issues; negative/toxic relationships; temptations; vices; abuse; weird power dynamics; resentment; revenge; sometimes actual satanic stuff, etc
- Overindulgence of pleasure
- Codependency; bondage; hedonism
- Dark and obsessive; manipulation and negativity; oppressive heavy energy
- A lot of times stands for somebody who's really struggling internally, feeling stuck, feeling trapped and helpless; struggling with mental health issues
- Can indicate connections to no good people
- Oppressive or restrictive situations like blackmail, slavery, etc.

◆ NOTES ◆

The Devil

◆ REVERSE ◆

PULLING AWAY FROM NEGATIVITY
RECOVERY FROM A BAD SITUATION
DETACHMENT
MENTAL ILLNESS

◆ INDICATIONS ◆

- Becoming self-aware and breaking or starting to attempt to break the chains
- Getting a new perspective on issues that you felt powerless to change previously; revelation; reclaiming power
- Overcoming addiction; freedom
- Pulling away from the negativity, trying to get to a better place/standing
- Trying to get away from a bad situation
- Fighting back against negativity, ex. misogyny, racism, etc.; "Let's make this toxic horrible shit end."
- Can indicate trying to not look like the 'devil'; trying to push away from situations that are perceived as bad/negative
- So tied to whatever they want their narrative to be; no capacity to free themselves from bondage, to see the light; lost cause; hopeless mental illness

◆ NOTES ◆

The Tower

◆ UPRIGHT ◆

CHAOS, DESTRUCTION, TEARING DOWN
SUDDEN UPHEAVAL, UNEXPECTED CHANGE
BIG TRANSFORMATION
LIFE-CHANGING THINGS

◆ INDICATIONS ◆

- Change thrust upon you; the rug being pulled beneath your feet; structures and foundations falling apart
- Big changes/transformations; big things coming to an end to start new bigger things; things crashing down very quickly; unexpected blow/disruption/shake-up; being thrust into a place of uncertainty
- Trying to shake things up, change things
- Life-changing things that heavily affect or impact you
- Drama; devastation, catastrophic event; chaos, fighting
- People stuck in a tower or in a way of being now gain new awareness and perspectives (tower is struck by lightning, bringing upon liberation)

◆ NOTES ◆

The Tower

◆ REVERSE ◆

INTERNAL OVERWHELM

AVOIDING CATASTROPHE

DELAYING THE INEVITABLE, RESISTING CHANGE

REBUILDING, RESTRUCTURING (THE SYSTEM, THE NARRATIVE, ETC.)

◆ INDICATIONS ◆

- Internal shock or overwhelm; internal jumble of conflicted feels
- Emotions felt are more intense than the reality that's going on; people freaking out in some kind of way
- Things are not what they seem
- Avoiding catastrophe; a disaster averted
- Rebuilding, restructuring after a bunch of drama; covering up of an issue or drama (cover-up), trying to rebuild a broken tower
- "I'm in trouble let me find a way to make it look different"; restructuring the entire scenario and setup
- At times can be a sign that you are resisting change or running from the necessary destruction and upheaval, it's time to turn and face it
- Tower moment has already happened, a reminder to let go and focus on creating something new, to build something new or different in place of what was destroyed as it was destroyed for a reason
- Can indicate Old drama resurfacing

◆ NOTES ◆

The Star

◆ UPRIGHT ◆

HOPE, PEACE AND CALM AFTER THE STORM
STARTING SOMETHING NEW
ATTENTION
EXPOSURE, VULNERABILITY

◆ INDICATIONS ◆

- Wishing on a star; praying; what people wish and hope for
- Can be destiny: it will happen
- Exposure card, popularity, celebrity; status/clout/fame chasing: "How can we get more clout, grow our names even more?"
- The public; the exposed; what is seen; vulnerability; something coming out and seeing the light of day
- Attention; confrontation
- Looking for attention (for help, validation, etc.)
- Calm oasis; peace and calm after the Tower card; optimism is restored
- Wanting to take a leap of faith and try something new; birthing a new idea
- Getting started on something; starting something new; moving on to something new; getting new experience out of this; newness coming to you or that can come to you (emotion-wise, awareness-wise, etc.)

◆ NOTES ◆

The Star

◆ REVERSE ◆

NOT HAVING FAITH
UNABLE TO START SOMETHING NEW
NEGATIVE ATTENTION
NOT EXPOSED (TO PUBLIC, TO OTHERS, ETC.)

◆ INDICATIONS ◆

- Negative attention, embarrassment, like someone setting somebody up to get hated on; negative exposure, like bringing someone down from the star
- Celebrity that's exposed, at a disadvantage
- Too much attention
- Not having an identity or identity crisis
- Things done outside of what is seen; nobody knows
- Not having faith that things are gonna get better, feeling like things are not moving forward; diminished hope
- Not being able to start out on something; feeling like they can't move forward (with what they know, etc.); wanting to start something new but they can't
- Can indicate fear of being vulnerable and being yourself
- If beside 5 of swords, means end of existence

◆ NOTES ◆

The Moon

◆ UPRIGHT ◆

SECRETS, LIES, DECEPTION
HIDDEN AGENDAS AND MOTIVES
FEARS AND ILLUSIONS
UNKNOWN, MYSTERY

◆ INDICATIONS ◆

- Secrets, deceit, deception, lies, hidden emotions
- Smokescreen (something used as an excuse or front)
- Fears and illusions
- Done in secret; suppression
- Hidden agendas, motives
- Unknown/hidden things; things/people are not what they appear to be; not currently known to the public
- Subconscious, deep dreams
- Mystery; under the cover of the night

◆ NOTES ◆

The Moon

◆ REVERSE ◆

TRUTH COMING TO THE SURFACE
GAINING CLARITY, SEEING THROUGH THE ILLUSION
HONESTY
OVERCOMING FEAR OF THE UNKNOWN

◆ INDICATIONS ◆

- You can see through it (the lie, deception, etc.); no more hiding
- Exposing of secrets; someone uncovers or will uncover something that was not previously known; all the dark coming into light
- Something/things coming out in the open; truth comes to the surface
- More is going to come out (about that matter, that idea, etc.)
- Honesty
- Fear has vanished and able to proceed with confidence

◆ NOTES ◆

The Sun

◆ UPRIGHT ◆

HAPPINESS, SUCCESS
OPTIMISM, VITALITY, JOY
ILLUMINATION, CLARITY
CHILDREN

◆ INDICATIONS ◆

- Optimism; success; joy; enthusiasm
- Happiness; vitality; YES!
- Illumination, shedding light on something, seeing everything clearly
- Truth revealed
- Lots of great opportunities; positive sign
- Growing and being happier
- Being connected with your inner spirit; innocence and purity; can indicate having personal connection with someone
- May also pertain to kids

◆ NOTES ◆

The Sun

◆ REVERSE ◆

UNHAPPINESS
LACK OF SUCCESS AND VITALITY
SOMETHING THAT INITIALLY LOOKED GOOD BUT FELL THROUGH
LACKING LIGHT, THE NEED TO SHED LIGHT ON SOMETHING

◆ INDICATIONS ◆

- Unhappiness; falling out; lack of success, depressed life force
- Issues with connections; bond that is not healthy
- Something that's looking like it was going to be good but taking a big nosedive
- There was so much potential to be had here, but it fell through, like something that should have or is expected to happen, but it didn't happen
- Things in the dark
- Things will be okay but there's a need to shed light on something; a not so great situation but it could be turned into a better one
- Can indicate unexpected secret coming to light
- May represent negative things about/involving children/youth

◆ NOTES ◆

Judgement

◆ UPRIGHT ◆

REBIRTH, RISING TO THE CALL
ANNOUNCEMENT
PUBLIC, JUDGEMENT
FACING THE FIRE

◆ INDICATIONS ◆

- Judgment/decision coming from a place of clarity and composure, a blend of intuition and intellect; having pure intentions; on the right path
- Judgement day; seeking some sort of justice; people speaking out or feeling motivated to speak out about something; wanting to make things right
- Facing the fire, facing the judgement
- Public opinion; the public; public will be watching; too many people watching
- Other people; care/concern about other people's view; trying to look good
- Something has to end; may symbolize passing (of someone); offering/getting forgiveness
- Rising to the occasion and following the calling; finding your calling
- Experiencing a rebirth/resurrection, getting on your feet
- Can represent some kind of announcement

◆ NOTES ◆

Judgement

◆ REVERSE ◆

NOT LOOKING GOOD IN THE PUBLIC'S EYE
BAD REPUTATION, REFUSAL TO HEAR THE CALL
ERROR IN JUDGEMENT, OFF THE CORRECT PATH
NOT READY FOR SOMETHING TO END

◆ INDICATIONS ◆

- A critical error in judgment; not being objective or not following your inner guidance; refusal to hear the call
- A poor decision made and suffering the consequence/s of that
- Things that were not on the right path; something being off of the correct path; things that were not what we had in mind; something you're considering doing that's off-path for you; a no good option
- Feeling embarrassed especially in terms of the public's view; threatening/trying to embarrass/humiliate someone; can also mean being misrepresented
- Being overly critical or judgmental; can also be harsh or unfair judgement
- Has reputation of being a bad apple or has history of doing this 'bad thing' before
- Getting out of a situation of judgement (e.g., court case, prison)
- Resistance and rejecting the status quo or what is judged as the normal standards or public ideals; alienation
- Can indicate it wasn't the person's time, he wasn't ready

◆ NOTES ◆

The World

◆ UPRIGHT ◆

COMPLETION, CLOSURE OF A CYCLE
WHOLENESS, INTEGRATION
RESOLUTION
GLOBAL, OUT OF COUNTRY LINES

◆ INDICATIONS ◆

- It's over; things will end; wanting things to be over
- Ending/Completion of a cycle; it's the finality of a situation in your life, can be a job, a period of uncertainty or you putting your foot down and defending or standing up for yourself so fiercely that everything comes full circle; tying a bow on something
- Closure of old cycles, old mentality
- Can indicate resolution of problem/s, e.g., aiming or wanting to solve something, having found solutions to issues, someone else had to solve their problems, etc.
- A sense of wholeness and completeness
- A global thing
- Out of state, out of country lines, cross country lines

◆ NOTES ◆

The World

◆ REVERSE ◆

NOT OVER, UNFINISHED BUSINESS
CYCLICAL
FEELING INCOMPLETE, STAGNATION
CAN POTENTIALLY IMPACT THE WHOLE WORLD, TRAVEL ISSUES

◆ INDICATIONS ◆

- Unfinished business; something that's been going on for a while, cyclical
- Not over, this is not the last we're gonna hear of this
- Lack of completion; there are still fine tunings and details that need to be taken care of; loose ends
- Feeling trapped or 'not done' (e.g., feeling like the situation is unfair, etc.), hence not allowing things (or the cycle) to end
- Something that has the potential to impact the whole world
- Travel problems; delay in plans

◆ NOTES ◆

Ace of Swords

◆ UPRIGHT ◆

CLARITY
DECISION MAKING
BREAKTHROUGH
OPPORTUNITY

◆ INDICATIONS ◆

- Having to make decisions; new decision
- Opportunity brought to attention: "I see a new opportunity I'd like a challenge"; opportunistic behavior
- Moving forward; pushing forward with something
- Truth coming out; trying to move forward with the truth; wanting to make things right, figure things out
- Cutting through the misinformation
- Truth being a double edged sword; something that can be a double edged sword, ex., something that is a blessing and a curse
- The upright sword is symbolic of the mind and the intellect. At the tip of the sword is a wreath, indicating success and victory, and a crown, indicating mental clarity
- Logical Thinking, intelligence; ideas
- Raw power; victory; breakthroughs; clarity
- People who are ruthless in their thinking, like lawyers

◆ NOTES ◆

Ace of Swords

◆ REVERSE ◆

DECEPTIONS
IRRATIONAL OR CLOUDED JUDGEMENT
REGRET
MISSED OPPORTUNITIES

◆ INDICATIONS ◆

- Not being able to come out with the truth
- Lies, deceptions; faulty, wrong; hiding truths
- Seeing things with cloudy judgement
- Mental aggression, blockages or stress
- Missed opportunity
- Regrets, e.g., regret from a past connection; a mistake
- Not wanting to move forward because of the idea of things being a double-edged sword
- Power plays that turn ugly
- Not wanting to use resources in a good way; fighting unfairly
- Defeat, losing, not getting what you want on certain issues
- Also legal card

◆ NOTES ◆

Two of Swords

◆ UPRIGHT ◆

STALEMATE
DIFFICULT DECISIONS, COMING TO CROSSROADS
OPPOSITION
DIVISION

◆ INDICATIONS ◆

- Stalemate, indecision

- Fork in the road

- Having to make a decision; ultimatum

- Weighing in on a decision we can't go back from, e.g., permanent separation

- Ostracizing one person

- A pendulum swing

- Conflict between 2 choices, head and heart in conflict.

- Vision problems

- Waiting, contemplation

- What does my inner knowing tell me

◆ NOTES ◆

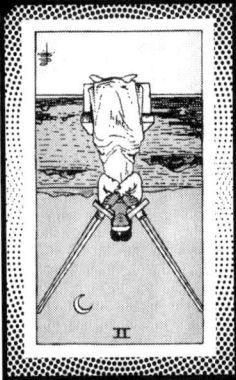

Two of Swords

◆ REVERSE ◆

DECISION MADE
SEPARATION
UNEVEN, UNBALANCED
TRUTH REVEALED (NOT BLIND ANYMORE)

◆ INDICATIONS ◆

- Decision is made

- Seeing the light; blindfold removed

- Not confused/bogged down anymore; not on standstill anymore; movement at last

- Able to see exactly what needs to be done

- Not torn, being able to commit to things and not be afraid

- A decision we can't go back from, like how a line is drawn and we can't go back

- Decision already made for us and we can't exactly get what we want; path has already been chosen, path already set

- Separate, separation, wanting to separate (also upright)

- Uneven, unbalanced

◆ NOTES ◆

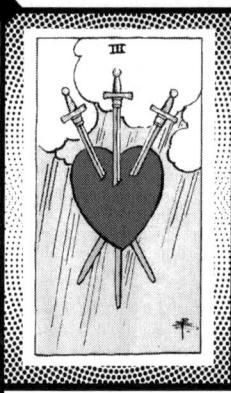

Three of Swords

◆ UPRIGHT ◆

HEARTBREAK
HURT, UPSET
BETRAYAL
SADNESS, GRIEF

◆ INDICATIONS ◆

- Heartbreak/breakup, really don't want this change, sad to see you go
- Loss, devastation, disappointment something you want to cry about, grim moment, sadness/depression over something
- 3rd party, somebody being left out in the cold; relationship comes to an end
- Experiencing deceit or deceiving someone; trifling behavior
- Feeling hurt; pain; despair; grief; sorrow; rejection
- Health: major surgery, actual cutting on the body
- Nailed to the cross, like "you're not allowed to do this anymore"
- Something being squashed, e.g., stopping information from coming out

◆ NOTES ◆

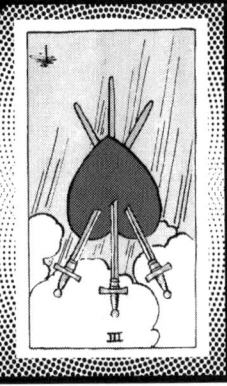

Three of Swords

◆ REVERSE ◆

RELEASING PAIN
OVERCOMING GRIEF/ SADNESS
NOT CARING
MITIGATED SORROW

◆ INDICATIONS ◆

- Releasing pain; letting go; forgiveness
- The storm is parting and the silver lining arrives; the dark cloud lifts
- In certain ways, the worst is over
- A problem that is smaller than it seems
- Reconciliation, healing
- Wanting to prevent heartbreak
- 3 people are/were involved
- Can mean not caring, or not gonna have time to care
- Can indicate stuff from the past that were very hurtful

◆ NOTES ◆

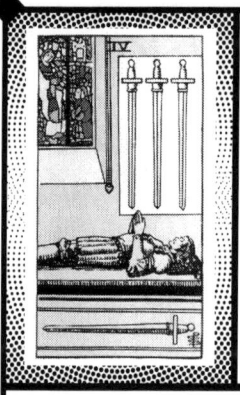

Four of Swords

◆ UPRIGHT ◆

REST, HEALING
CONTEMPLATION
RETREAT, LAYING LOW
PERIOD OF QUIET

◆ INDICATIONS ◆

- Needing to rest, chill, retreat, reflect; let your mind settle down; take a break from thinking, from strategizing
- Lull period; withdrawal, taking time off, vacation
- Healing of wounds, resting, grieving process
- Contemplation, recuperation, passivity, relaxation
- Something being laid to rest, put to bed; letting it go under the radar; a hideout
- Pulling away from something, trying to get as far away from it as possible
- Not talking about something for some period of time; staying close, laying low
- Can also be rejection, some kind of failure
- Succession (ex., grandfather, father are criminals, and you're going in the same path)

◆ NOTES ◆

Four of Swords

......................◆ **REVERSE** ◆......................

RE-JOINING THE WORLD, COMING OUT OF ISOLATION
BURN-OUT, RESTLESSNESS
NOT ACCEPTING
NOT HEALING

..........◆ **INDICATIONS** ◆..........

- Ending time-out
- Exposure, come out of hiding
- Feeling overwhelmed and burnt out by what's going on, not being able to relax from the situation
- Not healing; not feeling sorry; not grieving; unrest
- Rejection that somebody didn't take well, butthurt
- Not taking no for an answer, not wanting to fail, not wanting to go down, e.g., people trying to protect their assets
- Something that won't be gone for long and will be back up in a different way; unable to get rid of something or someone
- Forced to lay low or hide in some way
- Being isolated involuntarily
- Forced restrictions like telling someone "you can't do this, you can't do that"
- Can indicate talking about somebody's passing

..........◆ **NOTES** ◆..........

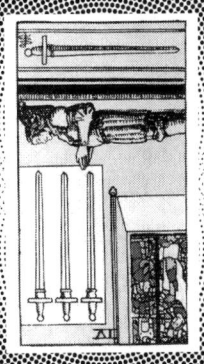

Five of Swords

◆ UPRIGHT ◆

CONFLICT, DISAGREEMENTS
COMPETITION
WANTING TO WIN AT ALL COSTS
OBSTINANCE

◆ INDICATIONS ◆

- Mindframe of "I want to win at all cost, gotta do what I gotta do by all means" (even if it's through unfair methods or even if it comes at a high price)
- Conflict of interest, tension, bullying, tit for tat
- Somebody playing mind games, throw others off their balance
- Unfair advantage; sore winners; dirty tricks
- Obstinance, fixed/stuck (in a certain mindset, etc.)
- When we are experiencing a conflict of ideas and expectations, it may not be helpful to have this confrontation, not worth your time to engage with a closed, stubborn mind
- Mental issues, mental insecurity; somebody wanting to prove that they're better, to feel validated
- Petty issues (also reverse); someone who's petty, feels ostracized and pushed to the side and wants to prove themselves
- All the little details

◆ NOTES ◆

Five of Swords

◆ REVERSE ◆

WALKING OUT
CUTTING LOSSES
INACCURATE DETAILS
TRYING TO GET AWAY

◆ INDICATIONS ◆

- Tired of 'this crap', wanting to disassociate or currently disassociating (e.g., from the situation, person, etc.); letting go and walking away from how something used to be; parting ways; throwing my sword down

- Trying to walk away from something; "I'm gonna separate myself from this and I'm gonna save my ass"; jumping ship, damage control

- Issues with details, stories, having inaccuracies in them, certain things missing, cherry picking, nitpicking

- Deceitful strategies that involve details

◆ NOTES ◆

Six of Swords

······················· ◆ **UPRIGHT** ◆ ·······················

CALMER WATERS
MOVING AWAY/FORWARD
CHANGE, TRANSITION
TRAVEL, DISTANCE

········ ◆ **INDICATIONS** ◆ ········

- Passage, progress, moving towards something
- Travel, change, distance; moving from 1 thing to another; transitional state; opportunities
- Peace, restoration, healing process; moving away from turbulent waters into calm waters, moving into a better place
- The internet (e.g., saying some stuff on the internet), use of internet and social media
- Coming out in the internet (info, news, etc.); information traveling fast
- Trying to better their path/situation, moving from rocky waters to smoother waters (e.g., using something or someone for one's gain)
- Related to transporting or trafficking
- Overseas (e.g., money/help/resource from overseas)

········ ◆ **NOTES** ◆ ········

Six of Swords

◆ REVERSE ◆

RESISTANCE TO CHANGE
STUCK, UNABLE TO MOVE FROM TROUBLED WATERS
RETURNING
CHALLENGES/HINDRANCES IN PROGRESS

◆ INDICATIONS ◆

- Resistance to change
- Things are not gonna get better (if you keep doing things that way)
- Traffic jam; no real movement/change; back to where one started
- Things not changing, transitioning or progressing in the best of ways
- Coming back; disrupted/cancelled travel; return from travel
- Not on the internet before
- Real life, not internet (drama, etc.)

◆ NOTES ◆

Seven of Swords

◆ UPRIGHT ◆

DECEITFUL, SHADY, SNEAKY
USING WITS, STRATEGIC
VICTORY THROUGH UNDERHANDED MEANS
GETTING AWAY WITH SOMETHING

◆ INDICATIONS ◆

- Shadiness, shiftiness, sneakiness; manipulating situations; making things fit where they don't necessarily fit; making themselves look good and get their way
- Someone who plots, plans, figures out what they need to do to get to where they need to get to no matter what it takes or the cause; victory through unethical or dishonest ways
- Feeling exiled, rejected; feeling they're not gonna get what they want so they resort to underhand methods; feeling paranoid and needing to twist things, cut corners in order to survive
- Someone who backdoors people; scoundrel, thief; lying, cheating, stealing; doing stuff behind your back.
- Something very strategic; can be a little bit secretive; moving silently; clever/strategic thinking, e.g., not sharing some things, plans or prospects to the wrong people
- Not all of it (e.g., information, resources, etc.)

◆ NOTES ◆

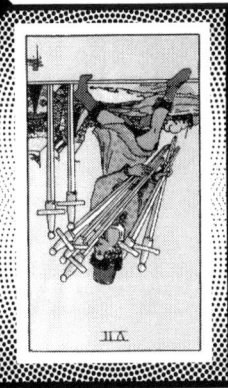

Seven of Swords

◆ REVERSE ◆

TACTLESSNESS, RUSE SEEN THROUGH
AVOIDING SOMETHING AT ALL COSTS
NOT WANTING TO BE INVOLVED
GUILT, WORRY, FAILURES

◆ INDICATIONS ◆

- Lacking strategy or failure in strategy
- Guilt, conscience; worried, wanting to stay in the shadows or hide
- Not wanting to be involved with something in any way; wouldn't touch "those swords" with a 10-foot pole; trying to save one's own ass (by trying to be heard, etc.)
- Can indicate separating/separated from something
- Not actually involved, but being implicated in something (or there is potential to be)
- "I don't know if I got what it takes, I don't know if I can do it."
- Imposter syndrome, self-doubt

◆ NOTES ◆

Eight of Swords

◆ UPRIGHT ◆

FEELING TRAPPED
RESTRICTION, IMPRISONMENT
VICTIMHOOD
ISOLATION, WITHHOLDING

◆ INDICATIONS ◆

- Bound, limitation; isolation; feeling stuck

- Victim of circumstance (also reverse), being pressured, trapped, cornered or pushed; if with 4 of wands, victim of their environment

- Screwing yourself over (e.g., overthinking, overcorrecting self, etc.); self-entrapment; perceptions of being imprisoned

- More trapped by fear than the actual thing/event

- Getting caught, being caught red-handed

- Restriction, restricted; hands tied

- Behind bars, jailed card

- Something's withheld; can mean 'wait'

◆ NOTES ◆

Eight of Swords

◆ REVERSE ◆

FREEDOM, RELEASE
FALSE VICTIMHOOD
GETTING AWAY WITH CRIMINAL ACTIVITY
RISING ABOVE LIMITS

◆ INDICATIONS ◆

- Trying to find a way forward, creating a new version of the future
- Trying to get out of victim mentality
- "We won't be victims anymore, we'll speak out, we're not gonna put up with this anymore."
- Trying to release self from shackles, from being entrapped, get out of a rough situation
- Can also be about the end of being tied up with something; hands not tied or full anymore; finally free to move about and do other things or what you want
- Somebody who considers themselves a victim when they're not actually
- Somebody who has done criminal/underhanded activity but they get away with it
- Can mean feeling hopelessly bound up, being in an uber sticky situation, feeling impossibly stuck and unable to let go

◆ NOTES ◆

Nine of Swords

······················· ◆ **UPRIGHT** ◆ ·······················

ANXIETY, WORRY
FEAR, DEPRESSION
REGRET, NIGHTMARES
STRESS, OVERANALYZING

············ ◆ **INDICATIONS** ◆ ············

- Overanalyzing, overthinking, getting stuck in our heads; too much identification with fear-based thoughts; reliving negative experiences
- Stress, regret, feeling bad
- Somebody who's in constant disarray, worrying over and over (how they're gonna go about something, get out of a situation, etc.)
- Obsessive or overwhelming thoughts, profound anxiety, sitting up at night pondering and reviewing; mental suffering; beating self up, a sense of shame
- Getting knifed in the back; feeling like the victim; can indicate illness, hospital stays
- Depression card; nightmare card
- Someone going out of their way to cause you pain or anguish; needing a ray of light to come into your life
- Someone who's not smart enough and ended up in a difficult or painful situation
- Can mean there is a person around you that needs your help/guidance

············ ◆ **NOTES** ◆ ············

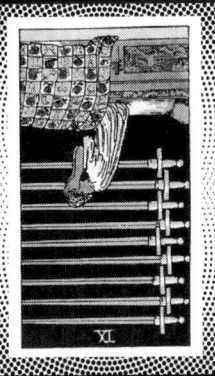

Nine of Swords

◆ REVERSE ◆

RELEASE OF ANXIETY
LETTING GO OF NEGATIVITY/STRESS
LIGHT AT END OF TUNNEL
PARANOIA, MENTAL HEALTH ISSUES

◆ INDICATIONS ◆

- Release of anxiety; dissipating of dark thoughts; letting go
- Freeing self; getting off one's own back
- Situation already remedied and already made amends for
- Something that could make people feel a little less anxious
- Someone who's not really fretting, not having sleepless nights or regrets about something or a certain situation
- Hopelessness; not able to see what you have; being unable to see your way out of situation; inability to see the light
- Paranoia involved, deeply anchored fear/s; freaking out, not knowing what to do or how to handle it
- Someone somewhat losing their mind

◆ NOTES ◆

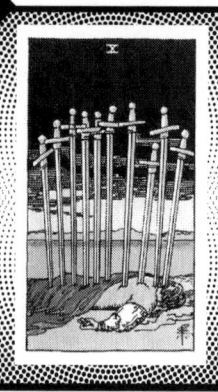

Ten of Swords

◆ UPRIGHT ◆

PAINFUL ENDINGS
BETRAYAL
RUIN, LOSS
SUDDEN, UNEXPECTED

◆ INDICATIONS ◆

- Painful ending, finality, defeat, failure

- Backstabbing, a betrayal, treachery, ruination at the hands of another

- Something came unexpected

- Devastation, crisis, hitting rock bottom

- There's gonna be something that will screw some people over

- The last straw that broke the camel's back, but then it's over, it doesn't get any worse

- Let the old die; surrender; accept that things are done and move on

- Release your attachment to wanting things to be a certain way and welcome new horizons

◆ NOTES ◆

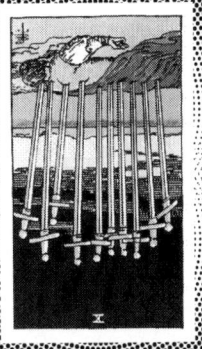

Ten of Swords

◆ REVERSE ◆

RESISTING AN INEVITABLE END
NOT WANTING TO LET GO
LETTING SOMETHING DRAG ON
SELF-SABOTAGE

◆ INDICATIONS ◆

- Resisting painful endings
- Taking things past their expiration date
- Not wanting to give up/let go (of your stance, position, etc.); not letting things come to an end when they need to come to an end
- Inadvertently making a situation worse for oneself, doing things that are potentially backfiring on you
- Self-sabotage, self-incrimination

◆ NOTES ◆

Page of Swords

◆ UPRIGHT ◆

INTELLECTUAL PURSUITS, NEW IDEAS
CLARITY
COMMUNICATION, MEDIA
PICKING UP THE SWORD TO FIGHT

◆ INDICATIONS ◆

- Opportunity to fight for, fighting for an opportunity
- About fighting, "I wanna fight"; wanting to create a fight; fighting tooth and nail for what is rightfully yours
- Useful info/important news coming forth, media
- Messenger of mental clarity: wake up, prepare to see or hear the truth
- Enlightenment, having a eureka moment about what happened and what's going on, knowing something about something
- Intellectual pursuits, ideas and reasoning
- Decision that they've put a lot of thought into
- Creative ideas, new ideas or new ways of thinking
- Situations that may demand sharp, critical thinking; needing to defend your thoughts or ideas
- Can also mean interception

◆ NOTES ◆

Page of Swords

············◆ **REVERSE** ◆············

NOT FACING THE FACTS
LACK OF CLARITY, CONFUSION
OPPORTUNITY NOT SEIZED
NOT FIGHTING THE BATTLE

·······◆ **INDICATIONS** ◆·······

- Not making sense, not being clear, confusing; something that's difficult to wrap our heads around
- Info or communication that lacks logic or isn't factual/truthful
- Opportunity not seized; opportunity not worth seizing, or not being able to step up to the plate
- People walking on eggshells around something and they're afraid to fight
- Putting down the sword, not fighting the battle, not gonna pick up the sword and swing; a battle not worth fighting for; as long as you don't fight fire with fire, you'll be fine
- Watching out for everything that happens, can be people put in places to spy on things, to see stuff that's going on and report back to somebody else; having some sort of insider info; watching/eavesdropping when they shouldn't be
- Page = something about kids; can mean immature thoughts; unwilling to face or speak the truth, resorts to lies or projecting onto others

·······◆ **NOTES** ◆·······

Knight of Swords

◆ UPRIGHT ◆

STRONG FORWARD MOVEMENT
CHARGING AHEAD
JUMPING IN, SWIFT ACTION
COMMUNICATION/INFORMATION COMING IN FAST

◆ INDICATIONS ◆

- Fighting forward, rushing forward, fast action, assertiveness
- Unexpected communication, air energy, something/someone came in fast, gave clarity to the situation
- Using a eureka moment to take some swift action
- Can generally pertain to thoughts, communication; working through stuff; making decisions
- Pure intentions, some sort of innocence
- Being some sort of 'hero', saving the day, helping or fighting for people; can be an aggressive attorney defending your case
- Requiring someone else to come in and save stuff
- If beside 8 of wands, someone who seems nice, but things changed

◆ NOTES ◆

Knight of Swords

◆ REVERSE ◆

NOT MOVING FORWARD
SCATTEREDNESS, RECKLESSNESS
BLOCKED TRUTH/INFORMATION
SELF-OBSESSED, VICIOUS

◆ INDICATIONS ◆

- Not moving forward, putting distance between self and something
- Not thinking clearly and rushing in to make decisions; regrets, poor judgement, scattered thinking
- Spiralling out of control mentally, freaking out a bit; unfocused mental energy, like a hamster wheel rolling; analysis paralysis
- Blocked communication, someone threw lies, deception, manipulation, harsh, ruthless communication; not telling the complete truth and giving a complete, clear picture, painting something that is one-sided or misleading
- Impure/bad intentions; spite work; "I am literally specifically targeting you"; a deliberate attack; act of vengeance
- Not a knight in shining armor, selfish; a person who may be trying to push their truth or worldview onto others; sometimes a mentally and/or physically abusive partner
- Can also indicate no one can help you or not wanting any help or not wanting to help someone anymore

◆ NOTES ◆

Queen of Swords

◆ UPRIGHT ◆

INDEPENDENT
LEVEL-HEADED JUDGEMENT
AWARENESS AND CLARITY
DIRECT COMMUNICATION, FRANKNESS

◆ INDICATIONS ◆

- Awareness, knowledge, sharpness
- Wise decision making; keen judgment; "gotta get smart about this"
- Level-headed; more thought-out vibe
- Sense of clarity and calm that comes from a clear mind; having a clear picture on what is going on and what to do.
- Making a choice to speak up about something, applying your integrity and common sense; no-nonsense, frank, logical approach
- Female air sign; a prominent female figure; cool, calculating, quick-witted, intellectual and clear-sighted; verbal; blunt energy; a very fierce and strong individual
- A period of strength while being by yourself; self-sufficiency; independence; self-reliance; can sometimes indicate breakup
- With Devil card, means standing up to something that felt oppressive to you, e.g., a situation where there is lack of communication, fairness, etc.
- Involving the law or lawyer/s

◆ NOTES ◆

Queen of Swords

◆ REVERSE ◆

OVERLY EMOTIONALLY INVOLVED
ALIENATED
RUTHLESS, BITTER, COLD-HEARTED
BLINDSIDED

◆ INDICATIONS ◆

- Having no idea, not really knowing what's going on, being blindsided
- Lacking awareness/knowingness and getting involved in a difficult situation that you cannot easily get out of
- If beside ace of cups, alienating the female that was around
- People talking crap, trying to isolate or push someone out; someone feeling alienated, sacrificed or pushed to the side
- This matter is completely out of the female or the individual's control
- May be thinking too much with your heart, and becoming too emotionally involved with your current situation
- Being catty, being too smart for your own good
- Can also mean being quite bitter, cold-hearted, or resentful; frigid; lack of compassion
- Can indicate ruthless energy: "I'll show you", vindictive, cutthroat, "I don't care"
- Someone who speaks with a forked tongue; backstabber; dishonesty; acting like they care but not really

◆ NOTES ◆

King of Swords

UPRIGHT

ASTUTE, STREET SMART
INTELLECTUAL POWER
AUTHORITY
LOGIC, REASON, LAW ENFORCEMENT

INDICATIONS

- Intellectual, clear, critical thinking; thoughts are communicated masterfully and intelligently; moving with insight; responds better to logic and well-thought out proposals
- Mentally sharp and tough; free of emotional clouds
- Verbal; witty but at times blunt
- Someone who is clever, book smart, street smart; very discerning
- Cutting through the BS
- Someone who has authority; powerful mind; great intellectual clarity, logic; can see big picture with great deal of understanding of the hows and whys of situation
- Can indicate someone who can be ruthless when dishonesty and illogical reasoning is detected
- Can be a lawyer, official, diplomat, scientist
- Truth seeker; fair judgement

NOTES

King of Swords

◆ REVERSE ◆

CONTROLLING, MANIPULATIVE
ABUSING ONE'S AUTHORITATIVE POWER
PETTY INTELLECTUAL ONE-UPMANSHIP
DECISION THAT ONE WILL REGRET LATER

◆ INDICATIONS ◆

- Selfish energy, insensitive, an opportunist; someone who's willing to do whatever it takes to get something; someone who's very complex internally
- Rigidness in thinking; controlling; tendency to over-control
- Tyrannical, abusive and cruel habits; may indicate the misuse of one's mental power, drive, and authority
- Con artist; employing dishonest approaches like persuasion and manipulation to fulfill selfish desires
- Showing off one's level of intelligence, e.g., using big words when discussing ordinary topics
- Intentions are impure; pushing someone out, deceptive legal maneuvers; someone who operates by a different code of ethics
- Leadership difficulties or issues
- Being too overly ambitious; lacking awareness; in over one's head; will regret this decision; not realizing what they're getting themselves into
- Can indicate not being interested in people that talk well and interested more in people that 'feel' well

◆ NOTES ◆

Ace of Wands

◆ UPRIGHT ◆

INSPIRATION, CREATIVE SPARK
NEW PASSION, ENTHUSIASM
NEW ENERGY, ACTION
BREAKTHROUGH, A FRESH START

◆ INDICATIONS ◆

- New action, new energy, new creative ideas (e.g., to get the job done, to approach a certain issue/situation, etc.)
- Brand new start, new door opening, starting something new; reboot, rebirth
- Birth of something new; a major offer or opportunity; career or moving forward in career
- A plan, project, etc. coming forward with inspiration, an a-ha moment or the arrival of inspiration/breakthrough
- Action taking place; green light
- An announcement, an offer or proposal
- Can be a phallic symbol; sex; pregnancy
- The seed of potential; potentially something new could occur

◆ NOTES ◆

Ace of Wands

◆ REVERSE ◆

DELAYS, BLOCKS
LACK OF PASSION, LACK OF ENERGY
UNABLE TO MOVE FORWARD
NOT NEW, RETURN OF THE OLD

◆ INDICATIONS ◆

- Whatever you or they're trying to start/restart, it's not gonna come to fruition; there may be something preventing it from happening
- Couldn't move forward; never had the chance, stunted, trapped; not able to move forward in the way you want
- Stuff is on hold; delays; can be a rejection notice; impotence (can be of a plan, possibility, potentiality of something, etc.)
- Miscarriage, fertility issues
- Return of an old idea; return of someone old
- An old problem; old issues you can't get away from; old flames returning
- This was planned for a very long time
- Past

◆ NOTES ◆

Two of Wands

◆ UPRIGHT ◆

PLANNING, MAKING DECISIONS
LEADERSHIP, GLOBAL
DOORWAY
FRICTION BETWEEN 2 PEOPLE OR ENTITIES

◆ INDICATIONS ◆

- Setting off on a new journey
- Doorway (exiting or entering, opening or closing)
- Split, crossroads, trying to pick between 2 ways
- Looking out the window, waiting to see what's gonna happen; trying to think big, looking out there, making plans (also reverse); deciding what we can do
- Step back and get an overview of what's going on
- World leadership, country leadership, leadership
- Dominion
- International/global thing, things/issues happening across the world
- Friction (between 2 people), fighting and conflicting energies, frustrations
- Can indicate inappropriateness; some sort of sexual advance/engagement

◆ NOTES ◆

Two of Wands

◆ REVERSE ◆

LACK OF PLANNING
DENIAL & FEAR OF DIRECT CONFRONTATION
OVERANALYZING
GOING BACK TO THE DRAWING BOARD

◆ INDICATIONS ◆

- Making new plans, replanning, regrouping; can be making bad plans or lack of proper planning
- "This no longer feels in alignment with me, I'm going to go make new plans and figure out something else."
- Looking out for something that doesn't really happen
- Can mean lack of vision, thinking small time; being afraid to take the leap forward; sometimes you just need to start and see where it takes you
- Deliberately picking fights and stepping on each other's toes; passive-aggressiveness, misguided aggression; some form of denial
- Trying to avoid the fight; not wanting to cause problems

◆ NOTES ◆

Three of Wands

◆ UPRIGHT ◆

EXPECTING SHIPS TO COME IN
COMING TO THE SURFACE (OF RESULT, ETC.)
OVERSEAS
3 PEOPLE INVOLVED OR MIDDLE MAN

◆ INDICATIONS ◆

- Expecting a certain thing to come out of something (what you're working on, etc.); expecting something to happen; waiting for your ships to come in; the possibility of things improving
- Waiting to see what will happen, looking at the next steps
- They used a middle man; someone in between
- 3 people involved (also reverse)
- Something from overseas; might be going overseas; having impact/influence across other places in the world
- Coming to the surface
- Coming from an outside source
- Can also mean liberation, feeling liberated; freedom; possibility for expansion

◆ NOTES ◆

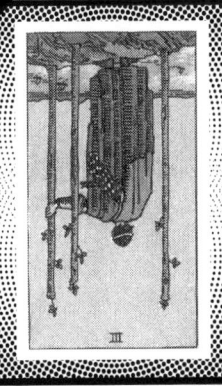

Three of Wands

......................◆ **REVERSE** ◆......................

ROADBLOCK
SHIPS NOT COMING IN
GETTING CAUGHT IN THE MIDDLE OF SOMETHING
EXPECTING SOMETHING DIFFERENT

........◆ **INDICATIONS** ◆........

- A wrench in the plan; not gonna happen; not permitted to continue; delays and setbacks
- This process is gonna drag on for a while, not entirely sure you're ready: still looking out if this is gonna be worth it, still considering the avenues available; reassessing
- Waiting out, not a whole lot moving forward on it just yet; not something that's taken off the ground just yet
- Looking out for something that doesn't really happen; expectations falling through
- Ships not coming in; things not coming to fruition in ways we were hoping it would
- "I was looking out for something else, I was hoping for something different."
- Getting caught in the middle of something; thrown from left to right
- 3rd hand involved
- A sort of liberation or something that seems freeing, but at a price, e.g., it's gonna affect their well being and emotional/mental health, etc.

........◆ **NOTES** ◆........

Four of Wands

◆ UPRIGHT ◆

CELEBRATION, JOY, HARMONY
HOME AND FAMILY
ENVIRONMENT SURROUNDING THE PERSON/SITUATION
MARRIAGE, FOUNDATION

◆ INDICATIONS ◆

- Pertains to the environment, surroundings
- Card about career and relationships
- Card about home and family; "we're in similar circle"
- Happy home and family; stability in home and relationships
- Wanting to preserve standing, livelihoods, their image/"look", etc.
- Window of opportunity, marriage, foundations
- Administration

◆ NOTES ◆

Four of Wands

◆ REVERSE ◆

LACK OF SUPPORT, INSTABILITY
LACK OF FOUNDATION
HOME CONFLICT OR TROUBLE
LOCATION CHANGE OR OUTSIDE THE ENVIRONMENT

◆ INDICATIONS ◆

- New environment (e.g., wanting to change the environment, change the system, etc.); change of environment; left the environment; location change
- Outside the environment
- Something that negatively affects families
- Trouble in paradise, rocky waters
- Not planning on laying a foundation, foundation is unstable
- Tainted, broken family, family type issue, breaking of relationship
- Dispute over home; issues in comfort or home environment (e.g., feeling invaded, lack of boundaries, etc.)

◆ NOTES ◆

Five of Wands

◆ UPRIGHT ◆

CONFLICT, ARGUMENTS
COMPETITION, AGGRESSION
SETBACKS, FRUSTRATIONS
STRIFE

◆ INDICATIONS ◆

- Slightly blocked by sth; setbacks

- Frustration

- Confrontation; going after 'them'

- Energies that feel like war, can be protests, riots, tensions, hostile energy

- Strife (like the new battling the old), fighting back against the herd

- Conflict; falling out (with somebody); arguing, fighting; causing drama

- Can pertain to people that will be angry: opposition, stress, chaos, push and pull

◆ NOTES ◆

Five of Wands

◆ REVERSE ◆

END OF TENSION OR VIOLENCE
TIRED OF FIGHTING
INNER CONFLICT
AVOIDANCE

◆ INDICATIONS ◆

- Gears starting to move (resolution of block or setback)
- Conflict in the past; restarting an old conflict
- Inner conflict (regret, etc.), inner conflicting feelings
- Wanting end of conflict/petty squabbles, tired of fighting and violence
- Struggle comes to an end or someone gives up and walks away, may be due to (the involved parties) being unable to come up to an agreement
- Avoidance, gonna avoid at all cost; needing to avoid or the avoidance of something (a certain person, group, confrontation, etc.)
- "We have to avoid this, shut it down."
- Tendency to deny and avoid something

◆ NOTES ◆

Six of Wands

◆ UPRIGHT ◆

TRIUMPH, VICTORY
REWARDS, RECOGNITION
EGO AND PRIDE
RIDING HIGH

◆ INDICATIONS ◆

- A win, feeling victorious; something you're really proud of; something that makes one feel good, successful; achievement; progress
- Center of attention, recognition
- Feeling some huge charge to do something about something; standing up for something (e.g., reform, change, etc.)
- Ego and pride; also a show card; a prideful type of person; ego boost
- Generally pertains to the ego, e.g. they're going to attack his character, his ego, confidence, etc.
- Wanting to look good, impress; being proud and standing tall
- Wanting to get back on your high horse, wishing we would be somewhere different

◆ NOTES ◆

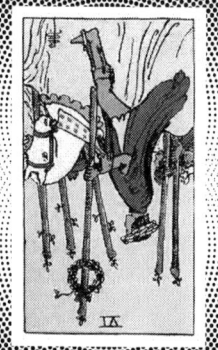

Six of Wands

◆ REVERSE ◆

FALLING OFF THE HORSE
LOSS OF PUBLIC FAVOR OR STATUS
HURT EGO AND PRIDE, HUMBLED
LACK OF RECOGNITION OR ATTENTION

◆ INDICATIONS ◆

- Falling off your horse
- A fall from grace, someone who's lost some sort of favor, clout, status, maybe job, camaraderie, support, social rank
- Regret; abandoning ship or a cause
- Bruised ego, in denial
- Feeling embarrassed, pride hurt
- Something that nobody paid attention to, not being seen
- Letting my ego/pride aside

◆ NOTES ◆

Seven of Wands

◆ UPRIGHT ◆

DEFENDING AND PROTECTING
STANDING UP FOR YOURSELF
UNDERDOG
HAVING THE HIGHER GROUND

◆ INDICATIONS ◆

- Standing up for what you believe in
- "I'm gonna fight, I'm gonna do what I can, I'm gonna fight for what I want"; not giving up; having the endurance to fight
- The underdog, having to prove oneself, have to prove something, e.g., one's innocence
- Fending off something (e.g., attacks/attackers, can be a way of being that doesn't serve you anymore; addictive tendencies, etc.)
- Trying to make sure that they'll be able to defend themselves; defensive posture
- Something they'll have to protect (so it doesn't get out there for example); doing some ass-covering and defending one's own position
- Having the higher ground, going in a unique direction especially with more integrity
- Can indicate the person will be fine in the end and will get over 'this situation', they're gonna retain their position, e.g., career will not be hurt, etc.

◆ NOTES ◆

Seven of Wands

◆ REVERSE ◆

CAUGHT OFF GUARD
GIVING UP
CAN'T PROVE, CAN'T MAINTAIN POSITION
UNWINNABLE

◆ INDICATIONS ◆

- Giving up, having to give up; emotional resigning, unplugging
- Not doing as well as they should be; scared, worried, don't know what's going on
- Can't prove myself, can't do anything
- "We can't fight for it"; something that's not winnable; need to let go
- Got caught off guard; one would have never expected it; weren't really prepared for having to deal with this: "Do I fold, what do I do?"
- Brought down from the higher ground by people with malicious intent: "You're pure, with integrity, let's corrupt you. I want you to no longer be an underdog."
- Not feeling the need to take a defensive posture: "I don't need to prove anything, I don't need to do anything."
- Not an underdog, cannot defend themselves, they did what they did
- Not supposed to be 'on the hot seat'; like, not technically a person's fault but he/she feels responsible or takes responsibility

◆ NOTES ◆

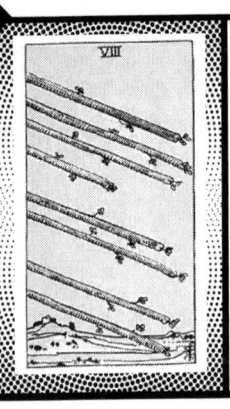

Eight of Wands

◆ UPRIGHT ◆

RAPID CHANGE
MOVEMENT AND ACTION
ACCELERATOR, CATALYZER
INFORMATION COMING OUT

◆ INDICATIONS ◆

- Rapid change; something moving (forward) very quickly
- Rapid communication, e.g., one day we're getting told this, next day we're getting told that
- Something or something that happens that will accelerate the movement, path, progress, etc.; accelerators, catalyzers
- Somebody holding some sort of receipts over another's head
- Social media; news spreading fast
- Some kind of communication/information coming out: texts, emails, phone calls being leaked, people ratting out somebody else, etc.

◆ NOTES ◆

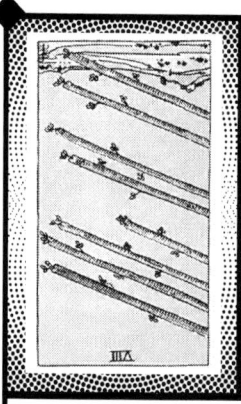

Eight of Wands

◆ REVERSE ◆

SLOW PROGRESS, DELAY
NOT MOVING FORWARD ACCORDING TO EXPECTATION
COMMUNICATION/INFORMATION ISSUES
EXPOSURE/S HANGING OVER ONE'S HEAD

◆ INDICATIONS ◆

- Windfall, unpredicted windfall; something not moving forward in the way that is expected, the way that maybe people would want it to; things aren't moving forward the right way
- Slowly changing, slowing down
- Communication going sour, communication issues
- Communication blocked/delayed; filibuster; receipts, communication, info getting screwed/going south
- Backing out of a situation; pulling back after some initial progress, e.g., person is now distancing himself
- Less communicable; failure of transmission in some way, shape or form (of info, disease, etc.)
- Some sort of negative receipt hanging over one's head; shady communication (like text messages, etc.); information brewing that hasn't been out there but might start creeping its way out

◆ NOTES ◆

Nine of Wands

◆ UPRIGHT ◆

RESILIENCE, PERSISTENCE
DEFENSE, BOUNDARIES
CHAOTIC DRAMA BEFORE THE SETTLING OF STORMS
HARDSHIP, WOUNDED

◆ INDICATIONS ◆

- Being defensive, standing your ground, holding your own, but covering your ass as well; ain't no one gonna take you down; "we build our fort and dare you come over here"
- Building up your defense, gotta be resilient; defending strength; determination; defiance
- Barrier, boundary
- Going to be a long fight
- Drama, chaotic storms, going or been through some shit
- Things getting worse before they get better; 9 = climax
- Nearly made it, you're nearly there; the final push
- Some kind of a hardship, feeling a bit battered and bruised, wounded/butthurt; getting overwhelmed and stressed out; school of hard knocks

◆ NOTES ◆

Nine of Wands

◆ REVERSE ◆

BATTLE WEARY
KNOCKED DOWN
TRYING TO AVOID A STORM
UNABLE TO DEFEND/HOLD UP

◆ INDICATIONS ◆

- Being beaten down and not being able to get back up from it; battle weary; feeling like the wind got knocked out of our sails
- Feeling unresilient; knocked down; having a hard time being able to pick themselves up; losing strength in this fight
- Not being able to keep one's "fort", e.g., pride, status, gonna have to admit being a bad person, etc
- Being done, passion no longer there
- Walking on eggshells (like knowing some chaos or drama is coming, or being unsure of doing something for fear of causing trouble); terrified to pull the trigger; involving some form of threat
- Wanting to avoid a shitstorm
- Everything that's consuming too much energy, you can see it now; letting down one's guard; dropping defenses and starting to trust
- Can indicate there's no beef or drama, or someone you haven't had beef with before

◆ NOTES ◆

Ten of Wands

◆ UPRIGHT ◆
BURDEN WORTH HAVING, HARDSHIP CLOSE TO AN END
EXTRA OR TOO MUCH RESPONSIBILITY
FEELING CALLED TO ACTION
HOLDING SOME FORM OF INFORMATION

◆ INDICATIONS ◆

- Responsibilities and burdens
- Hard work, taking on a lot; somebody having a lot on their plate
- A burden worth having; will take an awful lot of work but it's gonna pay off; wanting to put in some extra work; "if I do this, it's gonna pay off for me"; "we're gonna make it"
- Feeling called to action, a sense of purpose/responsibility
- Something that's been really hard is coming to an end so that something new can begin, it wasn't easy though
- Someone carrying a lot of information
- "I've been holding on to this (burden, info, situation, etc.) for a while."

◆ NOTES ◆

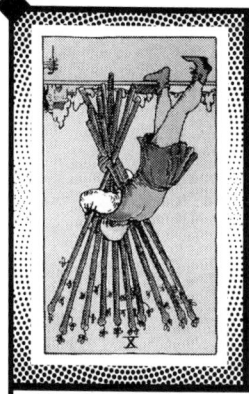

Ten of Wands

◆ REVERSE ◆

BURDEN NOT WORTH HAVING
RELEASED BURDENS OR BAGGAGE
BUCKLING UNDER PRESSURE
RESPONSIBILITY/IES BEYOND CAPACITY

◆ INDICATIONS ◆

- Burdens that are released; tired of 'this', wanting to lift burdens off one's back
- Liberation from something that feels heavy or oppressive
- Burden not worth having, e.g., thinking it would be like 'this', but it's not
- Taking on some things that are not gonna pay off; something they tried that's not paying off
- Extra responsibility that felt like it wasn't worth it
- Laying down the baggage and the bullshit, laying down the persona
- Not being able to hold up on the responsibilities and pressures
- Trying to do the right things yet it's not good enough or executed well or not applauded or acknowledged

◆ NOTES ◆

Page of Wands

◆ UPRIGHT ◆

MESSAGE ABOUT AN ACTIVITY OR ACTIONS
CREATIVITY, ENTHUSIASM
EXPRESSING ONE'S TRUTH
WHISTLEBLOWING

◆ INDICATIONS ◆

- Expressing myself and speak my truth, gaining a voice
- Speaking out; whistleblowing
- New creative expression
- Messages about actions
- Messenger card about creative projects or career; moving forward in career
- Enthusiastic, eager
- May be an opportunity that typically stems from or becomes a fight; can also represent a fiery or feisty child who loves physical activity and being on the go
- Can sometimes indicate spirit guides wanting to lay down a message; speaking through someone

◆ NOTES ◆

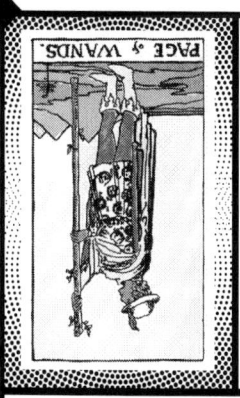

Page of Wands

◆ REVERSE ◆

LACK OF EXPRESSION OF TRUTH OR CREATIVITY
STIFLING OF INDIVIDUALITY
UNTRUSTWORTHY MESSAGE
HYPOCRISY

◆ INDICATIONS ◆

- Stifling your individuality, stifling your voice, your creativity; "I'm not speaking my truth, I'm not saying what I want."
- Manipulative how something's being presented; misinformation about something, not accurately conveyed
- Saying one thing and doing another; hypocrite
- You can't always trust the message; can't trust the message at face value
- Dishonesty; something that's done behind someone else's back
- Can indicate someone who knows the truth but will never tell

◆ NOTES ◆

Knight of Wands

◆ UPRIGHT ◆

FAST FORWARD MOVEMENT
PASSIONATE
IMPULSIVENESS, RECKLESSNESS
SOMEONE WHO ENTERS (OR LEAVES) QUICKLY

◆ INDICATIONS ◆

- Something coming forward very very quickly; something regarding communications that's getting out there fast
- There's action taken; direct laser focus on certain things
- Moving forward with vigor and/or enthusiasm; pushing forward as much as you can to get as much as you can
- Action and forward movement; moving things quickly; ducking in and ducking out
- Passion in relationships; passionate energy; very adventurous
- Someone who has a voice, not just a random person (e.g., someone who has a following, someone who has a role in making or influencing a decision about something, etc.)
- Moving forward without thinking well enough; can indicate a knee-jerk automatic real quick reaction
- Recklessness; immature dude; someone who tries to get in and get out hastily (also reverse)

◆ NOTES ◆

Knight of Wands

◆ REVERSE ◆

NOT MOVING FORWARD
SLOWING DOWN
HUSHED
VOLATILE, AGGRESSIVE, IMMATURE

◆ INDICATIONS ◆

- This forward movement has to stop; not wanting certain things to go forward
- Not moving forward, or maybe getting stuck in a situation and not knowing how to get out of it
- Can't rush this; not able to hurry something
- Low key and hush hush
- Making things slow down and reassess
- Getting cold feet
- Indirect (ex., attack, aggression, etc.)
- Having totally no idea that this is coming (e.g., went after the wrong person)
- Need to not fight back directly (especially with 7 of wands reversed)
- Something that feels more like a threat than an actual fall through (if beside 7 of swords reversed)
- Fuck boy card
- Being hasty about things; reckless, impulsive behavior; misguided aggression; temper tantrums; immature

◆ NOTES ◆

Queen of Wands

◆ UPRIGHT ◆

FIERY PASSION
SELF-ASSURED
WHOLEHEARTED
AMBITIOUS AND VIBRANT

◆ INDICATIONS ◆

- Confident, strong, courageous and intense; boldly expressing yourself; passionate about what one does

- Creative energy; in charge of their own life in their full glory

- Can indicate getting one's confidence back, stepping into one's power

- Go-getter, wholehearted type of energy

- Can be about an aggressive act; a little bit aggressive in chasing goals

- Can represent a beautiful, bold, feisty and sexy woman

◆ NOTES ◆

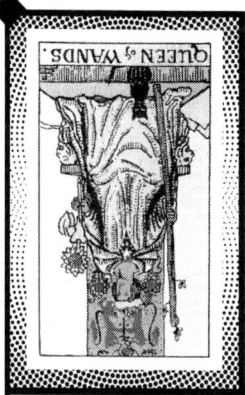

Queen of Wands

◆ REVERSE ◆

HOT-TEMPERED, MISGUIDED AGGRESSION
INSECURITY
EXCESSIVELY OR UNJUSTIFIABLY CONFIDENT
DEMANDING, VENGEFUL, BULLY

◆ INDICATIONS ◆

- Queen of wands is about fire energy, pushing forward, when reversed, there's some sort of reservation, holding back (something held back, delayed, stuck, needing resources, etc.)
- Someone needing affirmation/validation from others; insecure
- Confidence issues, not feeling confident about something or a certain direction
- Can also mean being overconfident
- "I create everything the way I want it to": card is reversed, that's not going to be the way things are
- Misguided aggression; someone who is angry and trying to push down their feelings
- Burning people out; not treating people right; pushy
- Lack of passion, care or enthusiasm
- Threat

◆ NOTES ◆

King of Wands

◆ UPRIGHT ◆

AN ENTREPRENEURIAL SPIRIT
WHOLEHEARTED ACTION
AMBITIOUS, A CREATIVE VISIONARY
POWERFUL, BOLD

◆ INDICATIONS ◆

- Action; passion; moving stuff around; being aggressive; chasing things
- Very dynamic; entrepreneurial; 'go go go' energy; able to motivate people
- Taking wholehearted action
- Powerful, strong, creative leadership
- Mature fire sign who is passionate, brave and commanding
- Very ambitious, very career-oriented, has a lot of things together and going for him
- People that follow things that come from the heart; maybe you're starting a new business or dealing with that fire energy
- Can be someone charismatic or well-known in the area
- Can sometimes indicate a new person or new management

◆ NOTES ◆

King of Wands

◆ REVERSE ◆

OVERLY AMBITIOUS
EXPLOSIVE EMOTIONS AND IMPATIENCE
IMBALANCED, FORCEFUL, ABUSIVE
INEFFECTIVE

◆ INDICATIONS ◆

- Irresponsibility; putting forth 0 effort; weak leadership
- A little too driven, unbalanced with their ambitions/passions
- Angry, hot-headed, blaming everyone; egomaniac; bully
- Misguided aggression
- Feelings of "I don't like how this is going. I need to figure out what to do so that I'm not floating around in this no man's land."
- Can sometimes indicate non-showy or indirect action/move, like, not wanting anyone to know

◆ NOTES ◆

Ace of Pentacles

◆ UPRIGHT ◆

FINANCIAL OPPORTUNITIES, MONEY
NEW JOB, NEW BUSINESS
OFFER, PROVISION
SOMETHING TANGIBLE (MONEY, DOCUMENT, ETC.)

◆ INDICATIONS ◆

- Money, finance; beginning of a new job; a new venture that is going to bring financial prosperity
- Pentacles = tangible, earthly things; in practical concrete terms, something new coming; a change in something
- More on the physical earthly needs as opposed to anything else; can be new person; something new that you can touch, use, etc.
- Gift of something new
- Can mean all about money, goals and gains, like aim or drive is all about gains; looking to get something out of 'this' financially
- Some form of tangible information/knowledge/receipt
- Some kind of offer or provision or wanting to provide
- A carrot dangled in front of someone; can be selling a story; can mean people following what's being given to them
- Can indicate ending up getting the money; won't lose the money
- If with Wheel of Fortune, money or resource coming out of nowhere

◆ NOTES ◆

Ace of Pentacles

◆ REVERSE ◆

LACK
ANY FORM OF LOSS
FAILED INVESTMENT OR UNABLE TO INVEST
HESITATIONS AROUND AN OPPORTUNITY/OFFER

◆ INDICATIONS ◆

- An opportunity delayed – or not as lucrative as originally thought; unexpected expense
- Feeling stressed out about money; money/financial issues
- Issues with the ability to do anything involving money
- Money wasted, time wasted; not achieving what I want to achieve
- Losing (job, favor from people, money, support/resource, etc.); lost of income/profit
- Something that could possibly cost them (not necessarily monetarily)
- Being not so sure about a certain gift/offer
- Not being able to invest totally in 1 thing
- Can sometimes represents lack; perceiving life or the world as lacking; feeling like what you have to offer is not enough
- Can indicate dubious ways of making a living

◆ NOTES ◆

Two of Pentacles

◆ UPRIGHT ◆

BALANCING TIME AND RESOURCES
JUGGLING (PRIORITIES, ROLES, ETC.)
SOME KIND OF EXCHANGE
TRANSFER OF MONEY

◆ INDICATIONS ◆

- Decisions, choices, balancing
- Pondering your options; balancing your time and resources and making ends meet; weighing your options; trying all kinds of things
- Juggling 2 sides; playing both sides
- A business move/exchange; a business decision
- Money going from one hand to the other
- Some kind of exchange: exchange of money or documentation or contracts (e.g., a deal, NDA, etc.)
- Giving information to someone (info going from one hand to another); sharing of information
- Collaboration between 2 people; something that benefits both people; "I scratch your back you scratch mine."
- Can sometimes indicate competition between 2 people: "2 can play that game."

◆ NOTES ◆

Two of Pentacles

················· ◆ **REVERSE** ◆ ·················

FAILURE TO JUGGLE
EXCHANGE OF HANDS OR DEAL FALLS THROUGH
UNEQUAL, UNBALANCED
INEFFECTIVE COMMUNICATION OR EXCHANGE

········ ◆ **INDICATIONS** ◆ ········

- Shows failure to juggle
- Imbalance; trouble managing your resources, time, or responsibilities; not able to make a decision or ineffective decision/s; unsteadiness
- Not being able to exchange hands; people pulling out
- Unequal exchange (e.g., something that's too expensive for the return; unfair/fishy deal, etc.)
- Improper exchange or exchange issues; not completely effective exchange of hands
- Can also represents wanting two-way communication with someone but not getting it

········ ◆ **NOTES** ◆ ········

Three of Pentacles

◆ UPRIGHT ◆

TEAMWORK, COLLABORATION
TANGIBLE IMPLEMENTATION OR RESULT
JOB-RELATED
SUPPORT

◆ INDICATIONS ◆

- Collaboration, teamwork, pooling resources and ideas; working together for a similar goal
- Great partnership/working relationship; getting support
- Having a meeting with regard to business, finances, etc.
- Tangible result card; your efforts will pay off; going to take time and effort; taking or needing to take action
- Represents job, money, status; can indicate job is fine or will be fine
- Can mean being really good at something, like being seen as an expert
- Can indicate a 3rd person who is in the situation

◆ NOTES ◆

Three of Pentacles

◆ REVERSE ◆

LACK OF COHESION OR TEAMWORK
ILL-INTENTIONED COLLABORATION
CONFLICT/EGO, DISSOCIATION
ISSUES WITH JOB, LACK OF EFFORT

◆ INDICATIONS ◆

- No sense of feeling collaborative; not playing well in the sandbox together
- Lack of effort/commitment; faulty plans
- Fighting, arguments, e.g., "you let us down"; ego clash; not trusting your partner's or teammate's ability
- Being really bad at something
- Collaboration that is not to be trusted; people involved who are up to no good
- Dissing or denouncing someone or a group; not wanting to associate with him/her/them
- Issues with job/career
- Can mean to the detriment of or at the expense of the project or one's job, e.g., pushing one's own agenda, sacrificing job for something or someone else

◆ NOTES ◆

Four of Pentacles

◆ UPRIGHT ◆

A NEED FOR CONTROL
GREED, MATERIALISM
HOLDING ON
FINANCIAL STABILITY

◆ INDICATIONS ◆

- Financial stability; financial acumen; possessiveness; protection
- Control, the need for it or trying to maintain control
- Holding on (to your pride, story, what doesn't work, etc.), holding on to emotions; guarded (shield around the heart); feeling a little too insecure to let go
- Holding on to something for dear life (e.g.; information, comfort, the old, etc.); desperately trying to cling to things to feel more in control
- Selfishness, greediness; dispute (e.g., protecting what's yours, "that's mine", etc.)

◆ NOTES ◆

Four of Pentacles

◆ REVERSE ◆

LETTING GO
GENEROSITY, GIVING TO OTHERS
FINANCIAL INSECURITY/ INSTABILITY
LACK OR LOSS OF CONTROL

◆ INDICATIONS ◆

- Letting go, release, opening up; sharing what you have; giving it all away; financial sacrifice
- Providing for other people, giving; "I've put so much time and money into you"; investing a lot of energy and resources in e.g., a relationship, cause, etc.
- Power grab; excessive control and greed; somebody who really likes their assets/money and they're really tied to that
- Some form of financial insecurity; issues with control over money, e.g., poor money management skills, not having full control over your finances, etc.
- So badly wanting control but not able to find resources (proofs, means, etc.)
- Losing control by trying to overcontrol a situation
- Make a desperate attempt at saving oneself
- Can indicate money/resources are gotten from someone else
- Potential blackmail

◆ NOTES ◆

Five of Pentacles

◆ UPRIGHT ◆

HARDSHIP, SHORTAGES
ISOLATION, FEELING ABANDONED
EXPERIENCE/POWER/RESOURCE DISCREPANCY
INSECURITY, POVERTY (OF FINANCES, WELLBEING, ETC.)

◆ INDICATIONS ◆

- Situation where one has power over someone or something (narrative, story, decision, etc.); money talks and power influences
- People that are taking more than they should; taking advantage of someone, energetically vampiring from someone
- Backed into a corner; thrown out in the cold; cut off; separation between 'them' and 'me/us' (social, financial status, etc.); blindsided; feeling left out, lonely or like a black sheep; excluded; abandoned
- People who are in a difficult or painful situation: livelihood, financial hardships, physical pains, etc.; feeling locked out from their blessings; needing stability
- Shortages, loss; setbacks, hiccups; running into difficulties
- Blockages, insecurities, coming from lack mentality; help is there but you are unable to see it; pity party; poverty consciousness; not feeling worthy
- Can represent information being iced out; not able to get the information through
- Can indicate apprenticeship; learning, growing; "I learn a lot from you so I'm around you"; people taking you under their wing; experience discrepancy; grooming someone to take the spot/position

◆ NOTES ◆

Five of Pentacles

◆ REVERSE ◆

IMPROPER OR ABUSIVE POWER DYNAMICS
JOB ISSUES, BAD BUSINESS DECISIONS
OVERCOMING ADVERSITY
RECOVERING FROM SOME FORM OF LACK OF RESOURCE/BENEFIT

◆ INDICATIONS ◆

- Messed up power dynamics, going about things the wrong way; weird power abuse, someone in the position of power and abusing it; controlling (also upright)
- Issues in career and job; power dynamic that is switched
- "I'm learning from the wrong people, I'm around the wrong things"; hiring someone you shouldn't have hired; shady hire; bad business decisions
- Someone or a group losing out and running out of the ability to make their way out of things through illegal or unethical means, e.g., bribery, paying their way out, etc.
- "You're not gonna keep me down and out"; somebody that has a point to prove
- Help arrives; ready to accept the help being offered; financial shift towards rebuilding; coming out of a hard time and starting again; leaving the mean streets
- When next to a judgement card, it's like you're telling the public that you're not involved: "I'm not with them"
- Can indicate getting close to being able to get some information through

◆ NOTES ◆

Six of Pentacles

◆ UPRIGHT ◆

GIVING AND RECEIVING
BUSINESS DEALS AND CONTRACTS
SHARING OR HANDING OUT
DEPENDABILITY, ACCOUNTABILITY

◆ INDICATIONS ◆

- Juggling finances, money coming in and also money going out; give and take; you had my back now I have yours
- Business deals, contracts, procedures
- Can also be a trust card, it's like, "you can depend on me"; dependability, accountability; consistency
- Sharing time, money, information
- Something being apportioned; who do we vouch for, who do we not
- Can indicate justice being doled out; things work themselves out
- Handing out (trinkets, welfare, aid, amnesty, etc.)
- Sharing the wealth or being in a position where you have to ask for assistance; "Can I have some of this money sir, can I have some, please?"
- Bird seed card, giving 'bird seeds' to 'birds'; breadcrumbing people

◆ NOTES ◆

Six of Pentacles

◆ REVERSE ◆

UNEQUAL EXCHANGE
SHADY DEALINGS
BREAKING OF DEALS OR CONTRACTS
UNRELIABLE

◆ INDICATIONS ◆

- Unequal exchange; giving more; not getting what's fair or deserved; imbalance like power imbalance, one is selfish and hoarding wealth, or one doesn't treat the other as well and the other is over-giving
- Holding back, like not wanting to say much and get in trouble because "I don't want to bite the hand that feeds me"; being in a bad position and no way out
- Bribes, blackmail, things like that
- Breaking of commitments, breaking trust, falling out, lack of follow through, no accountability
- Unreliable and breaking of contract, dissolving of a contract
- Can indicate past funneling of money

◆ NOTES ◆

Seven of Pentacles

◆ UPRIGHT ◆

WAITING ON RESULTS OR FRUITS OF LABOR
PERSEVERANCE, PATIENCE (EX., SAVING, RESERVING FOR NOW, ETC,)
LONG-TERM VIEW
COMFORT, KEEPING

◆ INDICATIONS ◆

- Work/Money-related; fruits (of labor) we're not fully seeing just yet; keep doing the good work
- Have to be patient, there are things you can't see yet; you can't do anything right now but let the seeds you planted grow
- Standing by, waiting on what's gonna happen (with this information, effort, turn of events, etc.)
- Compiling/accumulating more and more (evidence, resource, etc.)
- Enjoying the blossoming fruits of our labors; appreciating or assessing the progress
- Can indicate something they've been working on but has been buried for some time
- Can represent something that has been a long time in the making
- Can mean being comfortable; "I want to keep my comfort"; enjoying what's in front of you and how things are; "I have all these things and I want to keep them."
- Sometimes indicates complacency and laziness

◆ NOTES ◆

Seven of Pentacles

♦ REVERSE ♦

WASTE, LACK OF GROWTH
EFFORT OF FUTILITY
LACK OF REWARD
OUT OF COMFORT ZONE

♦ INDICATIONS ♦

- An exercise of futility; effort/work/career is futile
- Not able to see the potential; frustration with rewards; an unproductive investment; wasted energy
- Seeds planted are not growing; can be things that didn't get worked on or given half-assed effort
- Feeling powerless, like it's an effort of futility to get involved with this, anyone who gets involved in this will sink with the ship
- Out of your comfort zone; what's in front of you is not what you're expecting or are used to or comfortable with
- Impatience; inability to stand by and wait; giving up too soon

♦ NOTES ♦

Eight of Pentacles

◆ UPRIGHT ◆

CRAFT MASTERY, SKILL DEVELOPMENT
WORKING ON SOMETHING, PRODUCTIVITY
PERTAINING TO CAREER OR WORKERS
FRUITFUL EFFORT

◆ INDICATIONS ◆

- Card of apprenticeship; person learning their craft; making a mastery of something (doing it over and over again); practice makes perfect; person who has a little more experience in the matter
- Practice, things we want to practice
- Working on it; not an overnight thing, takes some time; working on things
- Focused on whatever you set your mind on; prolific; productive
- All the effort we put in
- Effort is rewarded
- Something that's pertaining to career
- Can represent the working people

◆ NOTES ◆

Eight of Pentacles

◆ REVERSE ◆

WASTED EFFORT
CAREER ISSUES
INEFFECTIVENESS OF SOMETHING
PRODUCTIVITY ISSUES

◆ INDICATIONS ◆

- Wasted effort

- Negative effect on career; something negative, bad or challenging about career; blows to their career; losing money

- Bad reputation or damage to reputation

- Something that's not working anymore

- Lack of effort/commitment/focus, poor quality; poor productivity

◆ NOTES ◆

Nine of Pentacles

◆ UPRIGHT ◆

INDEPENDENCE, SELF-SUFFICIENCY
FINANCIAL STABILITY, PROSPERITY
THE INDIVIDUAL, EVERY MAN FOR HIMSELF
RESOURCES UNDER ONE'S COMMAND

◆ INDICATIONS ◆

- Wealth and material comforts surround you; someone who has full control over their finances
- Having everything you could need or want
- Feeling better financially, fairly well-off female, benefit to us financially
- Happy, rich; "I'm making it work"; powerful; grounded; successful harvest; enjoying life's luxuries
- Individual; making money on my own; working alone
- Wanting to keep my business, my money, my assets in the way that I want
- Can indicate 'every man for himself' type of situation
- Someone isolating themselves, sheltering themselves

◆ NOTES ◆

Nine of Pentacles

◆ REVERSE ◆

LACK OF INDEPENDENCE/STABILITY/SECURITY
FINANCIAL DISTURBANCE, CAREER ISSUES
IMPROPER OR INCORRECT USE OF RESOURCES
RELATIONSHIP

◆ INDICATIONS ◆

- We're not the same career woman as we are before; I don't feel like I'm a master career woman right now; this is not my full expression, I could be doing something different; this career isn't doing it for me anymore
- Powerful female who's not using her power in the best ways; someone who has power but they don't know how to wield it appropriately; letting ego get in the way; using one's (plentiful) resources in unethical ways
- Something upset your financial security; something disturbed your finances, career
- Losing business; to not be able to go to work
- Can indicate being in relationship; other people; going to other people

◆ NOTES ◆

Ten of Pentacles

◆ UPRIGHT ◆

WEALTH, LONG-TERM SUCCESS
FAMILY, INHERITANCE
SUPPORT, PRIVILEGES, RESOURCES
COMMITMENT

◆ INDICATIONS ◆

- Wealth and prosperity, money (lots of it); very successful; long-term success; longevity; self-perpetuating wealth; legacy; something continuing; inheritance
- Financially or emotionally very grounded, very abundant
- Empire-building
- Commitment; can be marriage; business deal with positive outcomes
- Can represent some powerful people, maybe power couple
- Can indicate a lot of support, privileges, resources, etc.

◆ NOTES ◆

Ten of Pentacles

······················◆ **REVERSE** ◆······················

LONG TERM ISSUES, COMMITMENT ISSUES
HUGE LOSS OF MONEY, SUPPORT
THINGS FALLING APART, EMPIRE COLLAPSE
FOUNDATION, STATUS TAKING A HIT

········◆ **INDICATIONS** ◆········

- Long-term plan failed; long-term issues
- Something that could really disrupt career, cause people to lose (a lot of) money, support, backing, reputation, status, footing, public respect, etc.
- Not having enough experience
- Can indicate someone wants you to lose everything; someone doesn't want to see you successful or doing well or being happy/confident
- Breaking of bonds, commitment, relationships; getting a divorce; couples having problems; family problems
- Can indicate 'not for money', like they're not doing it or in it for money
- Can signify things not all coming in (e.g., not all the votes came in, maybe we lost some)
- Things falling apart

········◆ **NOTES** ◆········

Page of Pentacles

·········· ◆ **UPRIGHT** ◆ ··········

MESSAGE/INFO IN TANGIBLE FORM
ABOUT JOB/CAREER/PROJECT
FINANCIAL OPPORTUNITY
MEETING EXPECTATIONS

········ ◆ **INDICATIONS** ◆ ········

- Starting something new (business, projects, political scenes, etc.); new financial opportunities
- Slow-moving communication/message/opportunity; earth energy (Taurus, Virgo, Capricorn); takes some time to come in
- Good news about money
- Something to do with job/career/status/project; some sort of a project; money; drumming up sales; financial gain (coming from the situation, a certain move, etc.)
- Child with money, but can also pertain to documents
- About expectations (between 2 people, etc); meeting/exceeding expectations
- Can also represent a studious person who takes great responsibility in learning their craft

········ ◆ **NOTES** ◆ ········

Page of Pentacles

••••••••••••••••••••••••••◆ **REVERSE** ◆••••••••••••••••••••••••••

KEEPING SOMETHING TANGIBLE UNDER WRAPS
BLOCKAGES & FRUSTRATIONS AROUND MONEY OR A PROJECT
A LETDOWN, A PROMISING SITUATION DISAPPOINTS
UNABLE TO GET A VENTURE OFF THE GROUND

••••••••◆ **INDICATIONS** ◆••••••••••

- Goals that fall short; blockages and frustrations around money; investment/project/goal/work not going quite well or as planned; a venture not taking off the ground; financial/work/career issues; not able to take the project forward in the way we want to
- Losing money/support; having lost something out; strained business/working relationship
- Bad financial news
- Expectations are low; if beside 6 of pentacles, it means they are reliable as long as money is flowing
- Not worth the expectation or money, a letdown; a promising situation disappoints; falling short on expectations (e.g., couldn't be what someone wanted you to be);
- Something that people know about but they're not sharing; keep this tangible thing that you have under wraps
- Projects/agendas that were kept under wraps and that shouldn't be happening
- Can represent people someone had partnered with or had some sort of affiliations with in the past

••••••••◆ **NOTES** ◆••••••••

Knight of Pentacles

◆ UPRIGHT ◆

PLANNING, PREPARATION, GETTING ONE'S DUCKS IN A ROW
SLOW, STEADY, PATIENT APPROACH
CONSISTENCY
BRINGING FORWARD SOMETHING TANGIBLE

◆ INDICATIONS ◆

- Hardworking, practical, methodical; slow-moving knight but reliable in what they're trying to accomplish
- Slow process/growth, will take a while; taking a relaxed, patient approach
- Really trying to figure out what to do with something; planning; getting your ducks in a row, e.g., preparing resources, orchestrating an event or course of action, lawyering up, forming alibi, etc. (also reverse)
- Focused on reaping a reward for the effort; working "the land" and preparing for a big harvest; grounded, steady, safe; pentacle in hand symbolizes creation, seed, finances, resources
- Consistency, this has been happening consistently, like, you've witnessed this before, you've done this before; you've done it for a while
- Pertains to tangible things; somebody bringing forward more tangible things; bringing money, like, there's money involved in this
- Evidence (e.g., documents, body, etc.) being moved
- A job offer; something related to career

◆ NOTES ◆

Knight of Pentacles

◆ **REVERSE** ◆

SLOWLY DEGRADING
FALLING SHORT ON GOALS, INTENTIONS, PLANS
UNABLE TO PRESENT
UNSTABLE, UNRELIABLE, INCONSISTENT

◆ **INDICATIONS** ◆

- Trying to get ducks in a row but not doing so good
- Trying to get somewhere, prove something but not having the means to do so
- Things not working well; slowly degrading; things not happening the way they want it to
- Never got a chance to present (the info, material, etc.)
- Losing of a job; lazy; falling short; inept; dysfunctional; not doing the work; impatient, taking harmful shortcuts
- Inconsistency, e.g., with profit margin, return of investment, stories that are not 100% accurate, who you are (facades), etc
- A stubborn, inflexible man or mindset; stagnation

◆ **NOTES** ◆

Queen of Pentacles

◆ UPRIGHT ◆

SECURE, DEPENDABLE
SENSIBLE, GROUNDED
NURTURING, PRACTICAL PROVIDER
ABOUT MONEY, CAREER

◆ INDICATIONS ◆

- Secure, dependable, practical, self-made
- Can represent the support, mother figure
- Nurturing, warm, reliable and ready to lend a hand to anyone in need
- Pertaining to foundation; grounded vibe
- Can mean focusing on self; focused on money, career; getting confidence back; doing your thing
- Can indicate feeling pretty successful; job opportunities; relating to job, career
- Payday; someone having the inclination/orientation of: "There's money around this, there's money to be made here."
- Woman who knows more (about the situation, event, etc.)

◆ NOTES ◆

Queen of Pentacles

◆ REVERSE ◆

ISSUES WITH CAREER
LIMITED RESOURCES OR EXPERIENCE
UNGROUNDED, IMPRACTICAL
COMING OUT WITH SOME KIND OF INFORMATION

◆ INDICATIONS ◆

- Struggling financially; somebody trying to provide but not able to adequately provide
- Someone who doesn't have a big substantial financial backing; limited experience
- Lacking groundedness or foundation
- Losing out on certain issues; losing out in career; issues with career; something that's not good for career
- Feeling sick and tired of career
- Situation wherein a person or entity wouldn't give a someone (esp. a woman) credit for what she's established; not given what was due (money, credit, etc.)
- Coming out with some kind of information

◆ NOTES ◆

King of Pentacles

◆ UPRIGHT ◆

WEALTH, BUSINESS
STABILITY, SECURITY
PROMINENCE, ABUNDANT RESOURCES
POWER MOVES, POWER GRABS

◆ INDICATIONS ◆

- Authority; secure; good provider; father figure; paternal vibe
- Stability/career card, about being stable, committed, grounded in your energy; comfortable in your life right now when it comes to finances
- Having a lot of money and control over money; a very wealthy, powerful, successful individual
- A very prominent, strong individual who has solid foundation, creates and generates lots of income and has a lot of resources
- Can represent the business, business things
- Practical and grounded, may indicate normalcy, the normal energy
- Reaping your rewards; can mean money-motivated
- Power moves
- Can signify life partner energy, or message when it comes to life partnership

◆ NOTES ◆

King of Pentacles

◆ REVERSE ◆

NOT AS INVESTED
FINANCIAL MISMANAGEMENT, CAREER ISSUES
STUBBORN, IMPROPER USE OF POWER/WEALTH
NOT ABOUT/AFTER MONEY

◆ INDICATIONS ◆

- A stubborn, difficult man; inability to change direction, ain't budging; controlling; abuse of power
- Power grab; unscrupulous use of money/resources; trying to get somebody paid off or people bought out; getting money the sleazy way
- Bad business move; financial mismanagement
- Issues in career; someone in position not pleased
- Someone who is not as interested, not as invested, e.g., in it for the paycheck but not really liking the job, keeping someone for convenience, blah energy towards something or someone may have towards you
- Can mean nothing to do with money, not about the money

◆ NOTES ◆

Ace of Cups

◆ UPRIGHT ◆

NEW RELATIONSHIP, NEW BEGINNING
LOVING BONDS
ANY KIND OF CONNECTION
EMOTIONAL AFFECTATION

◆ INDICATIONS ◆

- A new emotional beginning; something new
- New relationship; new person that is coming along
- A new beginning in love; friendships
- A connection; people you are connected with, can be family, friend, affiliations, etc.
- Things that are emotional to us at some level; something that's going to pull at emotional strings
- Getting out the good word
- Elixir of life
- Heart opening, loving bonds
- Pardon; peace; joy; celebration; blessing
- Can indicate positive outcomes; things are going to get better emotionally

◆ NOTES ◆

Ace of Cups

◆ REVERSE ◆

SEVERED BOND
EMOTIONAL IMBALANCE, OVERWHELMING OR REPRESSED FEELINGS
BAD CONNECTIONS
SADNESS, PAIN, LOSS OF LOVE

◆ INDICATIONS ◆

- Severing/severed bond; wanting to get away (from a relationship, commitment, etc)
- Making the wrong connections
- Spilling/showing stuff about something that's emotional
- Weaponizing love
- Loss of love
- Being sad and upset, an emotional disappointment; feeling let down and depressed or blocked; emotional pain

◆ NOTES ◆

Two of Cups

◆ UPRIGHT ◆
UNION, PARTNERSHIP
CONNECTION, CLOSE BONDS
AGREEMENT
INTERNAL FORCES COMING TOGETHER (NO LONGER CONFLICTED)

◆ INDICATIONS ◆

- Connection and cooperation; meeting; alliance
- Relationships; any sort of (positive) partnership – friendship or even work-related; connecting and coming together for a cause; sharing a common goal
- At the heart of 2 cups is a union between 2 individuals, 2 entities, 2 companies, etc.; beneficial to all parties involved; source of support
- Loving bond; harmonious union; bond/connection between 2 people; partnered with someone
- Something that's agreed upon
- Can be coming together of internal forces (no longer scattered/warring)

◆ NOTES ◆

Two of Cups

◆ REVERSE ◆

SEPARATION, DISCONNECTION, DIVISION
COMPETITION, TENSION
DISPUTES AND ARGUMENTS
A NO GOOD UNION (UNFAIR, IMBALANCED, ETC.)

◆ INDICATIONS ◆

- Relationships take a difficult turn; communication breakdown; a separation is possible; disputes and arguments; unproductive meetings
- Disconnect between 2 people; breaking of a connection; severing of a bond; wanting to disassociate or stay away from a union or alliance
- Burning of bridges; "we're not friends anymore"; broken relationships; bad relationships; a no good union
- Not seeing eye to eye; something off or imbalanced within the relationship; can be messing up something relationship-wise
- Some sort of competition; 2 people on an even playing ground; rivalry
- Can sometimes represent a relationship from the past coming back

◆ NOTES ◆

Three of Cups

◆ UPRIGHT ◆

COMMUNITY, GATHERINGS
CELEBRATION
TEAM, SUPPORT
SOCIALIZATION, CONVERSATIONS

◆ INDICATIONS ◆

- Period of celebration; potential marriage; party
- Can indicate good news or good outcome, something to celebrate; good times
- The team
- The support surrounding you
- 3rd party or 3rd person involved (also reverse); socialization; can be somebody saying something behind your back, public will hear about it through whispers

◆ NOTES ◆

Three of Cups

◆ REVERSE ◆

GOSSIP, JEALOUSY
ISOLATION, FEELING CROWDED OUT
GROUP BEING AT A DISADVANTAGED POSITION
LACK OF SUPPORT

◆ INDICATIONS ◆

- Lack of celebration; group of people who are upset or something that will upset the group; the team being at a disadvantaged position (ex., losing, caught, etc.)
- 3's a crowd; lots of people involved; feeling crowded out
- May be somebody cheating; wandering eye; pulled a 3rd person into the loop; extramarital stuff
- Gossip and jealousy (can also be upright); distrust, disloyalty; issues with trust; heresay; not sure who you can trust
- Can indicate interference from an outside source; somebody interfering with the relationship (e.g., somebody who's trying to control the relationship, etc.); a lack of support; friends let you down
- Can mean standing out (e.g., not like the others, etc.)

◆ NOTES ◆

Four of Cups

◆ UPRIGHT ◆

DISSATISFACTION, DISCONTENT
HAVING TO ACCEPT AN UNPLEASANT OR UNPREFERRED SITUATION
REJECTION OF AN OFFER
DESPONDENCY

◆ INDICATIONS ◆

- Boredom, dissatisfaction; not happy with what's in front or what we've been dealt with or what's being offered; not getting what you really want; not liking what you're seeing/noticing
- Not really wanting something but having to just suck it up and deal with it or go with it
- Damned if you do damned if you don't, kinda feeling stuck in the situation (also reversed)
- Feeling like we're not really able to keep a hold on things in the way we're hoping for
- Things/actions that work in the past that are not working for us/them in the same way they used to
- Can be somebody from the past, somebody offering reconciliation, but you're like, "no!", ditching the situation; rejecting or pushing away an offer, etc.
- Sometimes pettiness
- Feeling a bit doubtful and discouraged, despondency
- Detaching from something; detachment; not caring; lack of empathy or sympathy (also reverse)

◆ NOTES ◆

Four of Cups

◆ REVERSE ◆

HAVING TO OR WANTING TO DETACH
DAMNED IF YOU DO, DAMNED IF YOU DON'T
DECISION RELUCTANTLY MADE OR MADE FOR YOU
FEELING LIKE HANDS ARE TIED

◆ INDICATIONS ◆

- A decision you wouldn't have wanted to make or be part of, but gotta do it, or it was made for you

- Apathy, feeling like hands are tied, having no choice, e.g., there's no real face-saving way out of this, a lot of damage already done, cannot put the genie back in the bottle

- Being forced to detach, e.g., detaching from the old

- Wanting to detach, detaching from someone/something, e.g., gonna force self out of the narrative, not giving a crap/shit about something that the public wants you to address, etc.

◆ NOTES ◆

Five of Cups

◆ UPRIGHT ◆

DISAPPOINTMENT, REGRET
FEELING DEFEATED
SORROW, GRIEVING, DEPRESSION
BITTERSWEET

◆ INDICATIONS ◆

- Disappointment (also reverse); feeling defeated

- Trying to pick up what was lost

- Moving through the grieving process; moving through pain

- Can indicate emotional instability, sometimes depression or resentment; feeling alone; crying over spilt milk; pity party

- Can mean bittersweet (like learning the truth but finding out that these truths are difficult to digest)

◆ NOTES ◆

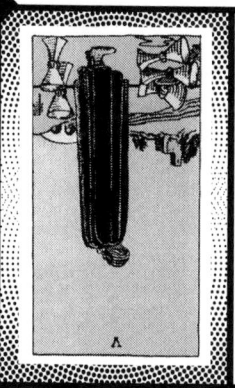

Five of Cups

◆ REVERSE ◆

PREDICTING DISAPPOINTMENTS
SILVER LINING
SALVAGING WHAT YOU HAVE LEFT
MOVING ON

◆ INDICATIONS ◆

- No longer disappointed, disappointment in the past
- Finally got to a place where you started trying to see things from a different perspective
- Can mean predicting disappointments, walking on eggshells, e.g., predicting someone getting emotionally overwhelmed and not being able to handle it
- Predicting the worst before it happens, like, viewing something as an issue/problem and creating problem out of it
- Trying to get out (of a situation) with the 2 cups you have still standing before the other 3 finish falling
- Trying to salvage what you have, trying to find some silver lining, trying to get to a better place
- Indicates there will be silver lining

◆ NOTES ◆

Six of Cups

◆ UPRIGHT ◆

PAST
KARMA
CHILDREN AND FAMILY
SOMEONE YOU HAVE HISTORY WITH

◆ INDICATIONS ◆

- Often represents the past; nostalgia, reminiscing; parents, childhood, origin; returning to one's roots
- Child and family card; sometimes marriage or proposal
- Living life from childlike wonder; blissful view
- People from the past coming back; someone you would have history with
- Karmic card (also reverse); karma will be served; what goes around comes around; you reap what you sow, you get what you deserve
- Some sort of release/launch (brand, product, etc.)
- May indicate being handed something by someone who has no authority (child giving something to another child)
- Having had a lot of (past) experience with something; an experienced person
- If with an Ace, it's like an offer coming that's restructured from the past

◆ NOTES ◆

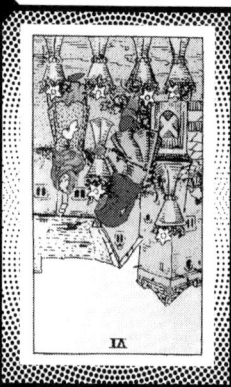

Six of Cups

◆ REVERSE ◆

STUCK IN PAST
DETACHING FROM PAST CONNECTION
FAILURE IN HANDING OUT/RECEIVING SOMETHING
CYCLIC PATTERNS

◆ INDICATIONS ◆

- Unwillingness to let go/move on; stuck in the past
- Grab from the past that might come forward; pushing out something that's from the past
- Can mean since they were kids; karma, cyclic patterns
- Mimics the past but it's different
- If with Page of Cups reversed, it means detaching from any kind of connection in the past
- Something that was not given and received, e.g., "they did not give me what was meant to be given to me"; can also indicate rejecting a gift/offer
- Something that negatively affects children/family

◆ NOTES ◆

Seven of Cups

◆ UPRIGHT ◆

FANTASY, ILLUSION, SMOKE AND MIRRORS
RIDICULOUS CLAIM, SHOCKING
LOTS OF OPTIONS, CHOICES
MULTIPLE POSSIBILITIES, OPPORTUNITIES

◆ INDICATIONS ◆

- Fantasy; something fluffed up
- Smokes and mirrors; illusion; shenanigans; confusion
- Ridiculous claim
- Can indicate one of many options; a lot going on; a lot still left to do/take care of
- Many possibilities/outcomes; things being able to go to a lot of different directions
- They got their hands on so many things; overwhelming/freaked out (also reverse); overwhelmed with different options
- Seeing something as a mixed bag
- Can mean something will be like a shock to the person

◆ NOTES ◆

Seven of Cups

◆ REVERSE ◆

CLARITY, SOBRIETY
REALITY REVEAL
BEING REALISTIC, SERIOUS
A CHOICE MADE FOR YOU

◆ INDICATIONS ◆

- Shattering someone's dream; things are not what they seem
- "I was sold a bill of goods that wasn't what I thought it was"
- Having the blinders/veil lifted and being awoken
- Dealing someone a dose of realism; bursting someone's bubble
- Things becoming clear; realizing/facing the uncomfortable truth of things: "Oh shit, this is too real."
- Being realistic, being serious
- Can indicate a choice made for you

◆ NOTES ◆

Eight of Cups

◆ UPRIGHT ◆

WALKING AWAY
ABANDONMENT
PUTTING DISTANCE
TURNING ONE'S BACK ON SOMETHING

◆ INDICATIONS ◆

- Able to walk away, out of choice; walking into a brighter day/place/scenario
- Walking away from something that doesn't emotionally fulfill you; moving on to better things
- Unplugging, disengaging and distancing self from something because of being fed up with it or not wanting to handle it; running away from issues (also reverse)
- Walking away temporarily; wanting to separate yourself from something, putting distance
- Pushing someone away, separating them, keeping them at arms length
- Abandonment; turning your back on something

◆ NOTES ◆

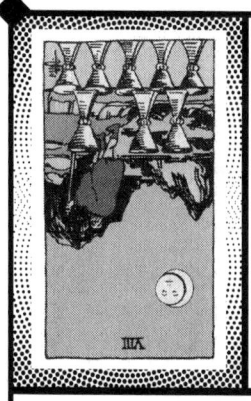

Eight of Cups

◆ REVERSE ◆

WALKING AWAY PERMANENTLY
EMOTIONAL DISTANCE
RUNNING AWAY, ESCAPISM
RETURNING

◆ INDICATIONS ◆

- Walking away permanently; permanent changes

- Whatever's gonna happen, it'll never be the same again

- Emotional distance

- Running away; avoidance

- Not time to walk away just yet; having to turn around and go right back

◆ NOTES ◆

Nine of Cups

◆ UPRIGHT ◆

WISHES COMING TRUE, MANIFESTATION
SATISFACTION, CONTENTMENT
PERTAINS TO WANTS, WHAT IS DESIRED
PROMISING BIG THINGS

◆ INDICATIONS ◆

- Wish fulfillment; manifestation of hopes and dreams

- Manifestation and getting what we want

- "I'm gonna get what I want and so I'm gonna do this"

- Someone promising big cool things, showing/saying what we want to see/hear

◆ NOTES ◆

Nine of Cups

◆ REVERSE ◆

UNFULFILLED DESIRES, UN-MANIFESTED DREAMS
NOT GETTING WHAT YOU WANT
GOT WHAT YOU WANT BUT IT TURNED OUT TO BE NOT SO GREAT
TROUBLE IN PARADISE

◆ INDICATIONS ◆

- Wishes unfulfilled; or you got what you wanted and it turned out to be not so great
- Trouble in paradise; not getting what you want
- Hope, wish and dream not gonna come true

◆ NOTES ◆

Ten of Cups

◆ UPRIGHT ◆

HARMONY, EQUILIBRIUM
HAPPINESS, EMOTIONAL FULFILLMENT
FAMILY
THE COLLECTIVE, GROUP, PEOPLE

◆ INDICATIONS ◆

- Happiness, joy; harmony; wholeness; completion
- There's a gift on the emotional level that's coming in; emotional fulfillment
- Family card (husband/wife, siblings); bond; life is looking good, particularly in domestic and family matters; connected to/concerning the family
- The community; gathering, groups, supporters, collective
- Something that will affect all people
- Can mean gaining/having understanding on the situation; can represent some sort of equilibrium
- Relating to a long-term goal/s

◆ NOTES ◆

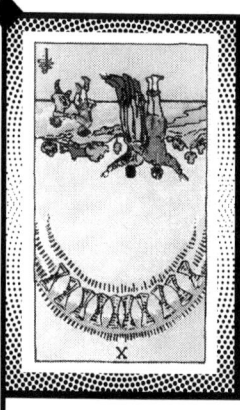

Ten of Cups

◆ REVERSE ◆

UNHAPPY HOME, DISHARMONY, DISAGREEMENTS
SEPARATION, ISOLATION
THE END OF A GOOD SITUATION
SOMETHING THAT NEGATIVELY AFFECTS THE COLLECTIVE

◆ INDICATIONS ◆

- Family troubles creating a crack in the foundation; squabbles and disagreements; no good home environment; the end of a good situation
- Something getting in the way of our "happily ever after"
- Not fitting in well; not meshing in well with the family; feeling separate from the family
- Breaking up of families; issue/s with families or close friends
- Can mean there's not a whole lot of ways for them to restore things
- Something that looks bad on the family

◆ NOTES ◆

Page of Cups

◆ UPRIGHT ◆

ATTACHMENT, CONNECTION
EMOTIONAL AFFECTATION/IMPACT
EMOTIONAL NAIVETY
FRESH EMOTIONAL START

◆ INDICATIONS ◆

- News that brings up emotions; messenger about emotional stuff; something that has an emotional impact
- Youth; starting something sentimentally new
- Trying to figure out the emotional implications, e.g., how is this person gonna react, how is this decision gonna affect me emotionally, what's in this for my emotional well being/satisfaction, is this worth involving myself in, etc.
- Someone trying to evoke an emotion out of you; someone wanting something: "Please sir, can i have some more?"
- Sensitivity and attachment; attached; can be somebody one is emotionally connected to; can be like an issue that you can't get away from
- Emotionally naive, emotional immaturity, lack of emotional intelligence; people who are acting young when they shouldn't be (also reverse)

◆ NOTES ◆

Page of Cups

······◆ **REVERSE** ◆······

BREAKING OF SENTIMENTALITY
EMOTIONAL IMMATURITY, CHILDISH
INSENSITIVITY, SELFISHNESS
SOMETHING UPSETTING (MESSAGE, ACTION, ETC.)

······◆ **INDICATIONS** ◆······

- Breaking of sentimentality, like friction with family; separating/detaching emotionally
- Not enjoying what's going on; something that would be upsetting; heart sink moment
- Somebody did them wrong emotionally
- There's an apology in order
- Somebody sending out messages that can defame someone's name; spreading some injurious or upsetting news
- Emotional immaturity; like creating a hissy fit; being overly sensitive
- Lack of emotional intelligence; it's all about 'me', what do 'I' want
- Insensitivity, lack of sensitivity; improper attachment/investment

······◆ **NOTES** ◆······

Knight of Cups

◆ UPRIGHT ◆

EMOTIONAL GROWTH, CARING, SENSITIVE
MOVEMENT/ACTION THAT ONE HOPES WILL (EMOTIONALLY) PAY OFF
MOVING FORWARD IN A WAY THAT FEELS GOOD
CHARM, ROMANCE, AN OFFER BEING MADE

◆ INDICATIONS ◆

- Leading with heart; taking action on feelings
- Wanting to go the way that we feel like is gonna emotionally pay off the most
- Emotional growth; growing up
- Knight in shining armor, charm, gentleness, romance
- Emotional investment, sensitivity and affection
- Can indicate feeling better emotionally
- Offer being made; bringing in something: invitation, info, etc.
- Something emotional coming towards you
- Things coming in to help with the situation

◆ NOTES ◆

Knight of Cups

◆ REVERSE ◆

IMMATURE OR EMOTIONALLY STUNTED
INSINCERE, DECEPTION AND MANIPULATION
SOMETHING THAT WAS INITIALLY APPEALING BUT TURNS OUT TO BE A BUST
EMOTIONAL TOLLS

◆ INDICATIONS ◆

- Immaturity; prematurity; cowardly behavior
- Not a knight in shining armor; someone who doesn't really have pure intentions
- Doing emotionally manipulative things; Not coming from a place of sincerity and true emotions or compassion (maybe thinking more on status, money, etc.)
- Not able to handle full-blown relationship
- Emotionally stunted; fueled by negative emotions or negative emotions blocking progress
- Emotional tolls, hurt feelings, sadness, pain, disappointment
- Can indicate that one is unable to come up with a face-saving way to resolve the situation

◆ NOTES ◆

Queen of Cups

◆ UPRIGHT ◆

COMPASSIONATE, CARING
EMOTIONALLY STABLE, INTUITIVE, IN FLOW
SUPPORT, NOURISHING
EMBRACING FEELINGS AND EMOTIONS

◆ INDICATIONS ◆

- Empathic, caring and sensitive, deeply nurturing
- Most psychic and intuitive queen; highly attuned emotional intelligence
- Support; mother figure or feminine energy
- Potential for things to be very loving
- Overall result of something is good
- Can indicate going to some sort of care

◆ NOTES ◆

Queen of Cups

◆ REVERSE ◆

IMPROPER OR LACK OF EMOTIONAL INVESTMENT
COLD, EMOTIONALLY MANIPULATIVE
OVERLY-SENSITIVE, INSECURE, NEEDY
SOMETHING THAT'S NOT REALLY SUPPORTIVE OR NOURISHING

◆ INDICATIONS ◆

- Being completely out of touch with your feelings or everyone else's
- Not 100% emotionally secure
- Emotionally manipulative; emotional attachment
- Cold, unemotional; self-centred
- Not emotionally invested in something; not wanting to invest in something emotionally
- Emotional pain
- Can indicate someone who steps up to be the mother figure (like a sister who's not supposed to be the mom); improper emotional investment
- Can mean the feeling will pass

◆ NOTES ◆

King of Cups

◆ UPRIGHT ◆

EMOTIONALLY STABLE AND MATURE
UPHOLDS VALUES AND MORALITY
COMPASSION, GENEROSITY, DIPLOMATIC
PERTAINS TO EMOTIONS OR EMOTIONAL INVESTMENT

◆ INDICATIONS ◆

- Nurturing, friendly; compassion, generosity; paternal energy
- Being in an emotionally charged place but it's stable and mature; not compromising one's values/standards; very good at calmly communicating what he wants, what he's hoping to achieve
- Emotional balance; knows how to manage his emotions; doesn't spew out on other people
- Someone people go to for comfort
- Altruistic acts; very good at making people feel that they emotionally care
- Can generally pertain to emotions; emotional attachment or connection
- Depending on other cards, can indicate feigning emotions (also reverse)

◆ NOTES ◆

King of Cups

◆ REVERSE ◆

EMOTIONALLY IMMATURE
EMOTIONALLY MANIPULATIVE OR ABUSIVE
UNCARING, UNKIND, COLD, REPRESSED
DRAMA KING

◆ INDICATIONS ◆

- Moody; unbalanced; emotionally manipulative; uses his ability to sense the emotional weaknesses of others as a weapon against them; takes advantage of vulnerability in others to get his own way
- Not emotionally invested; "I don't care anymore", does whatever he wants; selfish
- People who have no good intentions
- Someone who made/makes people feel like shit, pushed away
- Emotionally disconnected man; completely detached from anything; cold, aloof, lack of empathy; hollow, shallow energy
- Emotionally immature; overly emotional or too sensitive
- Sense of promiscuity; emotionally unstable

◆ NOTES ◆

Helpful Points

COURT CARDS

- King - Older male
- Queen - Older female
- Knight - Younger male
- Page - Younger individual
- Wands - Fire sign
- Pentacles - Earth sign
- Swords - Air sign
- Cups - Water sign

- King - power, authority, male/paternal energy
- Queen - nurture, support, female/maternal energy
- Knight - ambitious, forward-moving, assertive
- Page - messenger card, youth

UPRIGHT
- Positive qualities
- At an advantage
- Good intentions

REVERSE
- Negative qualities (extreme/excess or lack thereof)
- At a disadvantage
- No good intentions

ZODIAC ASSOCIATIONS

- Aries - The Emperor
- Taurus - The Hierophant
- Gemini - The Lovers
- Cancer - The Chariot
- Leo - Strength
- Virgo - The Hermit
- Libra - Justice
- Scorpio - Death
- Sagittarius - Temperance
- Capricorn - The Devil
- Aquarius - The Star
- Pisces - The Moon

GENERAL GUIDE

REVERSE	UPRIGHT	REVERSE
No - resisting (the upright meaning of the card) due to holding on, not being ready, event is accidental/unexpected so there's a lot of resistance, etc.	**Yes** - yes to the quality/meaning the card represents (that is the case)	**No** - not anymore, not the case anymore, can also be 'not worth' (the expectation, fight, etc.)
Lack	**Balanced**	**Extreme/Excess** - forced, forceful, too much at the expense of integrity, etc.
Past - something that's over/done, happened before, stuck and not letting go	**Present**	**Future** - predicting, trying to prevent, wanting, potential, etc.

Final Tips

- Prior to reading, some (including myself) set an intention of protection and ask the forces (forces of light, spiritual companions, etc.) to show only the truth. It's up to you if you feel the call to do this or how you wanna go about this. As for me I recite a single sentence and that's it. Others do more elaborate rituals. You can look into other sources for ideas. Again, always, it's up to you.

- Sometimes the card can indicate a literal representation. For example, a reading on a murder case where the Ace of Swords reversed came out. In that particular case, it represented a shovel pointing to the ground signifying the perpetrators used a tool to bury the body. So, be open, things like this can come up. Sometimes you'll also be drawn to a particular part/detail of the card image, which would represent what the card is trying to tell you.

- Have the phrases "as it relates to.." or "with regard to.." at hand when reading a spread. Read the cards considering their relationship with each other. Just as an example, let's say, the Ace of Wands, Queen of Pentacles and the Hanged Man. This would mean: this particular new idea/action (Ace) **as it relates to** the (male or female) querent's career (Queen of Pentacles) would have to or is going to be put on hold (Hanged Man). The Queen of Pentacles in this case just points to the 'career/job/business', and not specifically a 'dependable, nurturing woman'.

- Keeping a Tarot reading journal is an effective way to track the accuracy of your interpretations when doing divination readings. Documenting your divination readings allows you to match your interpretations with the actual unfolding of events, so as to develop a personal familiarity and connection with the cards and get to know the corresponding realities they tend to represent in your readings. Keeping records enables you to build your own personal card meaning database, helping you to be more versed in future readings.

- Be light, easeful and have your own spiritual autonomy. Tarot is a tool, not a crutch. In the end, you have your own natural intuition, connectedness and flow. 'Right' actions and decisions happen even without consulting the Tarot. And even if 'not so right' decisions are made, as they inevitably will be made, see them from an integrative perspective, they serve us in some way, shape or form. Opportunities to learn and grow, to embody our deepest insights in the face of challenges and the unknown. :)

Notes

Notes

Notes

Notes

Notes

Notes

We hope you enjoyed this publication!

Check out our Tarot journals at
http://mysticalgarden.weebly.com/tarot-journals.html

Printed in Great Britain
by Amazon